access to geography

This book is due for return on or before the last date shown below.

Hodder & Stoughton

A MEMBER OF THE HODDER HEADLINE GROUP

034 080 0313

Acknowledgements

To Mary, Courtenay and Christopher

The front cover illustration shows an emigrant and child, travelling from eastern Brazil to the western frontier, reproduced courtesy of © Stephanie Maze/Corbis.

The publishers would like to thank the following individuals, institutions and companies for permission to reproduce copyright illustrations in this book: © Paul Guinness, pages 29, 43, 80 and 100.

The publishers would also like to thank the following for permission to reproduce material in this book: extract from *The Economist Newspaper*, 15 November 1988 © The Economist Newspaper Limited, London, 1988; extract from *The Economist*, 11 March 2000 © The Economist Newspaper Limited, London, 2000; extract from *The Economist*, 2 September 2000; extract from publication by Government Statistical Service, Government Office for London and the London Research Centre Crown copyright material is reproduced with the permission of the Controller of HMSO and the Queen's Printer for Scotland; extract from the article 'The 10 families of man who settled Europe are revealed in gene test' by Roger Highfield in *Daily Telegraph*, 10th November 2000 © Telegraph Group Limited 2000; Dr Shirley Zangwill for the extract from *The Melting Pot* by Israel Zangwill, 1908.

Every effort has been made to trace and acknowledge ownership of copyright. The publishers will be glad to make suitable arrangements with any copyright holders whom it has not been possible to contact.

Paul Guinness MSc is Head of Geography at King's College School, Wimbledon.

Orders: please contact Bookpoint Ltd, 130 Milton Park, Abingdon, Oxon OX14 4SB. Telephone: (44) 01235 827720. Fax: (44) 01235 400454. Lines are open from 9.00–6.00, Monday to Saturday, with a 24 hour message answering service. Email address: orders@bookpoint.co.uk

British Library Cataloguing in Publication Data
A catalogue record for this title is available from the British Library

ISBN 0 340 800313

First Published 2002
Impression number   10 9 8 7 6 5 4 3 2 1
Year   2007 2006 2005 2004 2003 2002

Typeset by Fakenham Photosetting Limited Fakenham Norfolk.
Printed in Great Britain for Hodder & Stoughton Education, a division of Hodder Headline Plc, 338 Euston Road, London NW1 3BH by The Bath Press Ltd. Bath.

Contents

Chapter 1   Introduction   1

Chapter 2   Migration: definitions, typologies and theories   4
    1   Introduction   4
    2   Migration typologies   7
    3   Migration theories   10
    4   Recent approaches to migration   19
    5   Migration data   22

Chapter 3   A brief history of migration   25
    1   Introduction   25
    2   The diffusion of early humankind   25
    3   The development of empires   28
    4   Global migrations   30
    5   Rural to urban migration: a global
       phenomenon   38

Chapter 4   Internal migration in LEDCs   41
    1   Classifying population movements   41
    2   The causes of migration   45
    3   The characteristics of migrants   50
    4   The effects of migration   53
    5   Policies and planning   56
    Case study: Internal migration in China   61

Chapter 5   Internal migration in MEDCs   69
    1   Introduction   69
    2   Urbanisation   69
    3   Counterurbanisation   72
    4   Internal and international migration   74
    Case study: Internal migration in Britain   75

Chapter 6   International migration   86
    1   Introduction   86
    2   Changing attitudes to migration   86
    3   The costs and benefits of international
       migration   88
    4   Global migrations   92
    Case study: The USA – international migration   98

Chapter 7   Refugees   106
    1   The establishment of the UNHCR   106
    2   The complexity of forced displacement   109

References   113

1 Introduction

'Views about migration and migrants are often based on the assumption of sedentarism, that populations used to be immobile and have been uprooted by economic or environmental factors. There is however much evidence to challenge this sedentary bias, and to view population movement as the norm rather than the exception'.

Arjan de Haan

The study of human migration is a multi-disciplinary field, being of interest not only to geographers and demographers, but also to sociologists, economists, historians and psychologists. Migration has been important in creating and sustaining a wide range of patterns of human activity. According to White and Woods (1980) there is only a limited number of questions to be asked concerning any particular migration phenomenon, whatever the disciplinary approach:

1. Why does migration occur?
2. Who migrates?
3. What are the patterns of origins and destinations and of the flows between them?
4. What are the effects on the areas, communities or societies that the migrants come from?
5. What are the effects of migrations on the areas, communities or societies of destination?

After fertility and mortality, migration constitutes the third component of population change. All three factors have a direct impact upon the size of a population. Fertility and immigration increase population while mortality and emigration result in a decline in population. These simple facts are summarised in the population equation

$$P = [B-D] + / - M$$

where P = population, B = births, D = deaths and M = migration. A population distribution map of the world or of any country or region is a reflection of past migrations as well as of the patterns of natural population growth both past and present. Of the three major components of population change, migration is the most difficult to conceptualise and measure as it is a physical and social transaction, not just an unequivocal biological event.

Migration has played a major role in shaping the global cultural map. The phenomenon is essentially a series of exchanges between places. The impact of migration on population change has been greatest where mass migrations have overwhelmed relatively small indigenous populations as exemplified by the demographic histories of parts of the Americas and of Australia and New Zealand. In turn the old colonial powers have relatively cosmopolitan populations compared with most of their non-colonial counterparts, as significant numbers of people from former colonies have sought a higher standard of living in the 'mother' country. The Afro-Caribbean and Asian elements of the British population are a reflection of this process. In countries such as Britain, France, Germany, Italy and the USA there is a considerable difference in ethnic composition between the large metropolitan areas and rural regions, as most immigrants invariably head for large urban areas where the greatest concentration of employment opportunities can be found.

Migration redistributes population. It is a key human response to imbalances in opportunities and resources. Its role in the processes of industrialisation and urbanisation is testimony to this fact. The degree to which redistribution takes place is influenced by a variety of factors which have changed in importance over time. In the earliest human migrations the physical dangers associated with the journey dominated the decision to move. As transport and other aspects of life became more commercialised, cost became a major factor. In the twentieth century legislation became the major obstacle to international migration as more and more nations put up legal barriers to immigration. Some countries, notably those in the former communist bloc of eastern Europe, also made it extremely difficult for their citizens to emigrate fearing that they would send back tales that the grass was greener in the West. Today the question of refugees and those seeking political asylum has become a major international issue, and a key area of policy difference for political parties in some countries.

Within countries, migration has been responsible for two major processes in the twentieth and twenty-first centuries – rural depopulation and counterurbanisation. Rural depopulation has affected both MEDCs and LEDCs alike while counterurbanisation has been largely restricted to the MEDCs. These processes have in fact become major political issues in some areas. Population decline in rural areas invariably results in service decline which can have a huge impact on the lives of the people remaining if key services such as schools and post offices are cut. Because the rural population in MEDCs is now such a small proportion of the total population, rural dwellers often feel that their voice goes unheard by government. Within commuting distance of large urban areas in the developed world, counterurbanisation became the dominant movement process in the latter part of the twentieth century. While counterurbanisation may benefit some of the established population in an area it can have adverse social, economic and environmental consequences for others. A significant economic problem is for young people in the established population whose access to the housing market declines as demand for property in the area rises.

International migration is strictly controlled by government policy. While countries differ in their willingness to accept newcomers, the idea of controlled entry is internationally accepted. However, control over internal migration is a different matter. There have been some examples of the direct control of movement, most notably the nations of the former communist bloc such as The Soviet Union and China. However, in the democratic world, governments have exerted a growing indirect influence on migration over the last 50 years through a variety of measures which include: regional policies, the construction of New Towns, the development of transport infrastructure, taxes on house purchase and planning restrictions.

Migration has been a major process in shaping the world as it is today. Its impact has been economic, social, cultural, political and environmental. Few people now go through life without changing residence several times. Through the detailed research of geographers, demographers and others, we have a good understanding of the causes and consequences of the significant migrations of the past which should make us better prepared for those of the future whose impact may be every bit as great. We can only speculate about the locations and causes of future migrations. Causal factors may include the following: continuing socio-economic disparity between MEDCs and LEDCs, global warming and all its implications, nuclear catastrophe, civil wars, and pandemics due to new diseases.

2 Migration: definitions, typologies and theories

1 Introduction

It is customary to subdivide the field of migration into two areas: *internal migration* and *international migration*. International migrants cross international boundaries; internal migrants move within the frontiers of one nation. The terms *immigration* and *emigration* are used with reference to international migration. The corresponding terms for internal movements are *in-migration* and *out-migration*. Internal migration streams are usually on a larger scale than their international counterparts.

Net migration is the number of migrants entering a region or country less the number of migrants who leave the same region or country. The balance may be either positive or negative. Some countries like the USA have always had a positive migration balance, whereas other nations, including Britain, have had a more varied migration history. The terms *gross migration* or *population turnover* are used to refer to the sum total of people entering an area and leaving it during a given time period. Both the measures of net and gross migration are useful because they identify distinctive elements in the movement pattern. The relationship between gross and net migration is expressed in terms of the *efficiency of migration*. Migration is said to be efficient when the difference between gross migration and net migration is low, that is when there is a dominant movement in one direction. Migration is termed inefficient when the gap between gross migration and net migration is high, that is when the difference

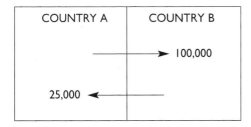

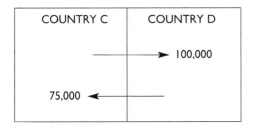

Figure 1 The efficiency of migration

between the number of people moving into and out of an area is less marked. In the simplified example shown in Figure 1 the efficiency of migration is high between countries A and B. In contrast the efficiency of migration between countries C and D is relatively low.

Migrations are embarked upon from an area of *origin* and are completed at an area of *destination*. Migrants sharing a common origin and destination form a *migration stream*. For every migration stream a *counterstream* or reverse flow at a lower volume usually results as some migrants dissatisfied with their destination return home. *Push and pull factors* encourage people to migrate. Push factors are the observations that are negative about an area in which the individual is presently living, while pull factors are the perceived better conditions in the place to which the migrant wishes to go. Once strong links between a rural and urban area are established the phenomenon of *chain migration* frequently results. After one or a small number of pioneering migrants have led the way, others from the same rural community follow. In some communities the process of *relay migration* has been identified, whereby at different stages in a family's life cycle, different people take responsibility for migration in order to improve the financial position of the family. Another recognisable process is *step-migration* whereby the rural migrant initially heads for a familiar small town and then after a period of time moves on to a larger urban settlement. Over many years the migrant may take a number of steps up the urban hierarchy.

Migration, like the other demographic variables of fertility and mortality, has crude rates. A *migration rate* is the ratio of migrants, observed or estimated, to the exposed population during a given time period. The *exposed population* consists of the initial population in the case of out-migration (the population at the beginning of the year in question) and the terminal population in the case of in-migration (the population at the end of the year in question). The four commonly used migration rates are as follows:

In-migration or immigration rate:

$$\frac{\text{The number of in-migrants or immigrants}}{\text{The exposed population of an area}} \times 1000$$

Out-migration or emigration rate:

$$\frac{\text{The number of out-migrants or emigrants}}{\text{The exposed population of an area}} \times 1000$$

Net migration rate:

$$\frac{\text{In-migration/immigration} - \text{Out-migration/emigration}}{\text{The exposed population of an area}} \times 1000$$

Gross migration rate:

$$\frac{\text{In-migration/immigration} + \text{Out-migration/emigration}}{\text{The exposed population of the area}} \times 1000$$

For a country with a population of 10 million, if 30,000 people left that country on a 'permanent' basis in a year and 50,000 entered the country on the same basis, then the migration rates would be as follows:

Immigration rate = 5/1000
Emigration rate = 3/1000
Net migration rate = +2/1000
Gross migration rate = 8/1000

In recent decades refugee movements have been considerable. *A refugee* is defined by the United Nations as someone who 'owing to a well-founded fear of being persecuted for reasons of race, religion, nationality, membership of a particular social group or political opinion, is outside the country of his (or her) nationality and is unable or, owing to such fear, is unwilling to avail himself (herself) of the protection of that country'. A distinction has been drawn between '*anticipatory*' and '*acute*' refugee movements. In the former, refugees have time to prepare in advance to leave their county or region while in the latter movement is much more immediate, with little or no time to make proper arrangements. An increasing number of people who have been forced to leave their homes do not in fact cross international borders. Such *internally displaced people* now come under the protection of the United Nations High Commissioner for Refugees (along with conventional refugees).

The term *evacuees* is often applied to people who have been displaced from their homes by such phenomena as natural disasters or infrastructural projects such as dam construction. *Resettlement* is the process whereby such displaced people are moved to a new location and, generally, given assistance by the government in order to maintain themselves there.

2 Migration typologies

Although the characteristics of human movement are complex, there have been various attempts to classify migration on the premise that classification is fundamental to a clearer understanding of the phenomenon. Such classifications are called migration typologies. The most important variables used in classifying migration have been:

* distance travelled
* the temporary or permanent nature of migration
* the causes of migration
* the selectivity of migration
* international as opposed to internal migration.

For example, Smith, after distinguishing between international migration and national migration, subdivided the latter into:

* rural to urban
* urban to rural
* state to state (region to region)
* local movement.

The Swedish demographer Hagerstrand (1957) arrived at a similar classification of:

Relation	Migratory force	Class of migration	Type of migration	
			Conservative	Innovating
Nature and man	Ecological push	Primitive	Wandering Ranging	Flight from the land
State (or equivalent) and man	Migration policy	Forced Impelled	Displacement Flight	Slave trade Coolie trade
Man and his norms	Higher aspirations	Free	Group	Pioneer
Collective behaviour	Social momentum	Mass	Settlement	Urbanisation

Figure 2 Petersen's migration typology
Source: Population Geography, Hornby and Jones

- urban to rural
- rural to urban
- rural to rural
- urban to urban.

In 1958 Petersen, in the American Sociological Review, noted the following five migratory types (Figure 2):

- The nomadic pastoralism and shifting cultivation practised by the world's most traditional societies are examples of *primitive migrations*, the outcome of people's relationships with their natural environment.
- The abduction and transport of Africans to the Americas as slaves was the largest *forced migration* in history. In the seventeenth and eighteenth centuries 15 million people were shipped across the Atlantic Ocean as slaves. In recent decades civil wars, particularly in Africa, have resulted in major refugee movements. Migrations may also be forced by natural disasters such as volcanic eruptions, floods and droughts or by environmental catastrophes such as nuclear contamination around Chernobyl.
- *Impelled migrations* take place under perceived threat, either human or physical, but an element of choice lacking in forced migration remains. Arguably the largest migration under duress in modern times occurred after the partition of India in 1947, when 7 million Muslims fled India for the new state of Pakistan and 10 million Hindus moved with equal speed in the opposite direction. Both groups were in fear of their lives but they were not forced to move by government, and small minority groups remained in each country.
- *Free migration* occurs when force or perceived threat are not factors in the migration decision. Here the potential migrant will weigh up a range of factors concerning both origin and destination before making a final decision.
- The distinction between free and *mass migration* is one of magnitude only with the former being small scale and the latter large scale. The movement of Europeans to North America was the largest mass migration in history.

Within each category Petersen classed a particular migration as either *innovating* or *conservative*. In the former the objective of the move was to achieve improved living standards while in the latter the aim was to maintain present standards.

Hagerstrand (1957), in his major study of Swedish migration fields, defined migration as the change in the centre of gravity of an individual's mobility pattern. In a local intra-urban move the destinations of the mobility flows need not change. However, in an inter-urban move they are likely to change. Roseman (1971) termed these two types of migration '*partial displacement*' and '*total displacement*' respectively.

Mabogunje (1970) differentiated between what he called *active and passive migrants*. The former are the initial risk-takers who set up

The vital transition	The mobility transition	

Phase A: *The pre-modern traditional society*

(1) A moderately high to quite high fertility pattern that tends to fluctuate only slightly
(2) Mortality at nearly the same level as fertility on the average, but fluctuating much more from year to year
(3) Little, if any, long-range natural increase or decrease.

Phase B: *The early transitional society*

(1) Slight, but significant, rise in fertility, which then remains fairly constant at a high level
(2) Rapid decline in mortality
(3) A relatively rapid rate of natural increase, and thus a major growth in size of population

Phase C: *The late transitional society*

(1) A major decline in fertility, initially rather slight and slow, later quite rapid, until another slowdown occurs as fertility approaches mortality level
(2) A continuing, but slackening, decline in mortality
(3) A significant, but decelerating, natural increase, at rates well below those observed during Phase B

Phase D: *The advanced society*

(1) The decline in fertility has terminated, and a socially controlled fertility oscillates rather unpredictably at low to moderate levels
(2) Mortality is stabilised at levels near or slightly below fertility with little year-to-year variability
(3) There is either a light to moderate rate of natural increase or none at all

Phase E: *A future super-advanced society*

(1) No plausible predictions of fertility behaviour are available, but it is likely that births will be more carefully controlled by individuals – and perhaps by new socio-political means
(2) A stable mortality pattern slightly below present levels seems likely, unless organic diseases are controlled and lifespan is greatly extended

Phase I: *The pre-modern traditional society*

(1) Little genuine residential migration and only such limited circulation as is sanctioned by customary practice in land utilisation, social visits, commerce, warfare, or religious observances

Phase II: *The early transitional society*

(1) Massive movement from countryside to cities, old and new
(2) Significant movement of rural folk to colonisation frontiers, if land suitable for pioneering is available within country
(3) Major outflows of emigrants to available and attractive foreign destinations
(4) Under certain circumstances, a small, but significant, immigration of skilled workers, technicians, and professionals from more advanced parts of the world
(5) Significant growth in various kinds of circulation

Phase III: *The late transitional society*

(1) Slackening, but still major, movement from countryside to city
(2) Lessening flow of migrants to colonisation frontiers
(3) Emigration on the decline or may have ceased altogether
(4) Further increases in circulation, with growth in structural complexity

Phase IV: *The advanced society*

(1) Residential mobility has levelled off and oscillates at a high level
(2) Movement from countryside to city continues but is further reduced in absolute and relative terms
(3) Vigorous movement of migrants from city to city and within individual urban agglomerations
(4) If a settlement frontier has persisted, it is now stagnant or actually retreating
(5) Significant net immigration of unskilled and semi-skilled workers from relatively underdeveloped lands
(6) There may be a significant international migration or circulation of skilled and professional persons, but direction and volume of flow depend on specific conditions
(7) Vigorous accelerating circulation, particularly the economic and pleasure-orientated, but other varieties as well

Phase V: *A future super-advanced society*

(1) There may be a decline in level of residential migration and a deceleration in some forms of circulation as better communication and delivery systems are instituted
(2) Nearly all residential migration may be of the inter-urban and intra-urban variety
(3) Some further immigration of relatively unskilled labour from less developed areas is possible
(4) Further acceleration in some current forms of circulation and perhaps the inception of new forms
(5) Strict political control of internal as well as international movements may be imposed

(a) The phases of the mobility transition and their relationship to the phases of the vital transition

(b) Changes in the volume of different kinds of mobility during the five phases of the mobility transition

Figure 3 The Mobility Transition hypothesis
(From P. Ogden: Migration and Geographical Change, CUP, 1984)

the line of communication between the rural and the urban area. This makes the journey between the two places and the process of settling down in the urban area significantly easier for those who decide to move at a later date (passive migrants).

While many other typologies have been produced, most do not differ significantly from the above and to include them here would add little to the discussion.

3 Migration theories

Since the latter decades of the nineteenth century various attempts have been made to develop models and theories of migration. The analysis that follows, although not exhaustive, attempts to set out the major developments in this theoretical work. The sequence presented is not entirely chronological, beginning with the very generalised concept of the 'mobility transition'.

a) Zelinsky's Mobility Transition

To place the variety of human migrations and their evolution over time in context the American geographer Wilbur Zelinsky (1971) proposed the notion of the 'Mobility Transition' (Figure 3). Here the intensity of different types of migration, (e.g. international, rural to urban), is related to stages of socio-economic development from the pre-industrial traditional society to a future super-advanced society. In Zelinsky's hypothesis the term 'circulation' covers a whole variety of movements (e.g. seasonal movements, journeys to work, holidays), not included under the general heading of migration. In Phase I there is very little real residential migration and a limited amount of circulation occasioned by social visits, the local economy, war and religion. Large scale movement does not begin to take place until Phase II when considerable rural to urban migration occurs alongside mass migration to new lands. In Phase III both rural to urban migration and emigration, although still important, are reduced to a lower level. New forms of movement begin to dominate in the 'advanced' society of Phase IV. Migrations between cities and within cities are now very significant along with much higher levels of circulation. On the international front the main movement is one of relatively unskilled workers from LEDCs to MEDCs. Phase V equates to the hypothetical fifth stage of demographic transition that now appears in many illustrations of the model.

Zelinsky explained how from the 'point of ignition in England' the desire to move 'outward or cityward' engulfed Europe in the nineteenth century and by the mid-twentieth century most other parts of the world. Thus, different countries pass through Zelinsky's phases at different times.

The Mobility Transition hypothesis can be criticised on a number of counts. As the idea is based on the histories of MEDCs it is not automatically the case that all LEDCs will follow suit. Cultural differences between nations are often important in fashioning 'progress'. Another criticism is the relative lack of explanation in a hypothesis which is largely descriptive. Surprisingly there is no reference to counterurbanisation, a major process in MEDCs over the last 40 years or so. It is also very unlikely that an advanced society would ever impose strict controls on internal migration. Nevertheless, despite some obvious limitations the Mobility Transition hypothesis provides a useful platform for discussion.

b) Ravenstein's Laws of Migration

Ravenstein (1834–1913) is recognised by many as the founder of migration theory. He was certainly one of the first academics to produce a list of broad generalisations concerning the character of migrants, their origins and destinations and the nature of migration streams which he referred to as his 'Laws of Migration'. However, Ravenstein himself recognised that 'laws of population, and economic laws generally, have not the rigidity of physical laws'.

He developed these ideas in three papers published in 1876, 1885 and 1889, basing his work initially on birthplace data for Britain in 1871 and 1881, but later including data from similar sources for North America and Europe. Ravenstein's first paper appeared in the Geographical Magazine, the other two in the Journal of the Statistical Society. This was a time of growing interest among the middle and upper classes in social conditions, education, public health and the developing science of economic and social statistics. In suggesting that the major causes of migration were economic, Ravenstein was echoing the eighteenth century political economists led by Adam Smith (1723–90).

Ravenstein's Laws of Migration may be stated as follows:

1. Most migrants move only a short distance. As distance increases from a particular place the number of migrants from that place decreases.
2. Migration occurs in a series of waves or steps. For example, the 'space' left by people moving from a market town to a city will be filled by people moving into the market town from its rural hinterland.
3. The process of dispersion (emigration) is the inverse of that of absorption (immigration) and exhibits similar features.
4. Each significant migration stream (flow) produces, to a degree, a counterstream.
5. The longer the distance travelled, the greater the likelihood of the destination being a major industrial and commercial centre.
6. Migrants are generally adults; families rarely migrate over long distances.
7. Town dwellers are less migratory than those living in rural areas.
8. Females are more migratory than males over short distances while males are more likely to move long-distance, particularly to other countries.

9. The volume of migration increases with the development of industry and commerce.

10. The direction of migration is mainly from agricultural to industrial areas.

11. The major causes of migration are economic.

Although Ravenstein was not without his critics at the time of publication, there can be no doubt that all of these assertions were valid, at least to a certain degree, in the latter part of the nineteenth century and that many of them are still relevant today. *Which of the hypotheses listed above do you think are the least relevant to the modern world?*

Although more than a century has passed since the publication of Ravenstein's work, theoretical advance has been limited despite thousands of subsequent migration studies. Later theoretical developments reinforced aspects of Ravenstein's work in some cases, and in others, modified it.

c) Zipf's Inverse Distance Law

Zipf (1949), using the concept of distance decay, presented the Inverse Distance Law, stating that 'the volume of migration is inversely proportional to the distance travelled by migrants'. This is expressed mathematically as:

$$N_{ij} \, \alpha \, 1/D_{ij}$$

Where Nij is the number of migrants from town i to town j and Dij is the distance between the two towns.

Thus, Zipf sought to explain migration by the 'principle of least effort' since the effort required to cover greater distances would presumably increase. In one of his analyses Zipf monitored the contents of the Washington Post, noting the locational origins of the news items carried. When he graphed the results it became apparent that there was a strong relationship between the distance from Washington to the location of the news item and the size of the location. Where locations were equidistant from Washington the larger locations featured much more frequently in the news, and for locations of the same size, those closer to Washington received more coverage. Thus the interaction (measured here by flows of information between places) is proportional to the size of places, and scaled down by their distance away.

d) The Gravity Model

The Gravity Model, which can not be attributed to one particular author, linked distance to the relative attractiveness of two places of different population size:

$$N_{ij} = k \, P_i \, P_j / D_{ij}^2$$

Here Nij and Dij are as for the Inverse Distance Law while Pi and Pj are the populations of towns i and j respectively; k is a constant. The model takes its name from Sir Isaac Newton's work on the gravitational field of the planets.

The Gravity Model is highly simplified as it assumes that each migrant has the same information available and that movement costs are the same in all directions. The decision-making process of the individual migrant is in effect reduced to a consideration of distance only.

The Gravity Model may be modified to include more sophisticated measures of the influence of the origin or destination or by substituting distance by road for a straight-line measure of distance. The Gravity Model has been used, in modified terms, by planners in a variety of fields.

e) Stouffer's Theory of Intervening Opportunities

In 1940 Stouffer, an American social psychologist, presented his Theory of Intervening Opportunities (later refined by him in 1960) in which he stated 'the number of people going a given distance is directly and inversely proportional to the number of intervening opportunities'. The formula is:

$$N_{ij} \alpha O_j / O_{ij}$$

Where Nij is the number of migrants from town i to town j, Oj is the number of opportunities at j, and Oij is the number of opportunities between i and j.

For Stouffer, linear distance was less important a determinant of migration patterns than the nature of the space. He regarded distance in socio-economic rather than geometric terms. Stouffer tested his theory on residential mobility in Cleveland, Ohio, and defined opportunities as the number of vacant houses (of a given rental group). He found that agreement between expected and observed values was high. Other researchers have tested Stouffer's model using job vacancies as the measure of intervening opportunities, arriving at equally good results.

f) Lee's Principles of Migration

Lee (1966) produced a series of Principles of Migration, in an attempt to bring together all aspects of migration theory at that time. Of particular note was his origin-intervening obstacles-destination model which emphasised the role of push and pull factors (Figure 4). Here he suggests there are four classes of factors which influence the decision to migrate:

1. those associated with the place of origin
2. those associated with the place of destination

Figure 4 Origin and destination factors and intervening obstacles in migration
Source: A Theory of Migration by E.S. Lee in Migration: Sociological Studies 2, edited by J.A. Jackson

3. intervening obstacles which lie between the places of origin and destination
4. a variety of personal factors that moderate 1, 2 and 3.

Each place of origin and destination has numerous positive, negative and neutral factors for the individual. What may constitute a negative factor at the destination for one individual, e.g. a very hot climate, may be a positive factor for another person. Lee suggested that there is a difference in the operation of these factors at the origin and destination, as the latter will always be less well-known, 'There is always an element of ignorance or even mystery about the area of destination, and there must always be some uncertainty with regard to the reception of a migrant in a new area'. This is particularly so with international migration. Another important difference between the factors associated with the area of origin and the area of destination is related to stages of the life cycle. Most migrants spend their formative years in the area of origin enjoying the good health of youth with often only limited social and economic responsibilities. This frequently results in an overevaluation of the positive elements in the environment and an underevaluation of the negative elements. Conversely, the difficulties associated with assimilation into a new environment may create in the newly arrived, a contrary but equally erroneous evaluation of the factors at the destination. The intervening obstacles between the origin and destination include distance, the means and cost of transport and legal restraints (mainly in the form of immigration laws).

There has been considerable debate about whether push or pull is more important in the decision to migrate. For example, Bigsten (1996) argues that the pull of high wages is more important than the push of land scarcity in explaining migration decisions in Kenya, while Adams (1991) finds the reverse in international migration from Egypt.

Lee used the origin-intervening obstacles-destination model to formulate a series of hypotheses about the volume of migration, the development of stream and counterstream, and the characteristics of migrants.

(i) Volume of migration

1. **The volume of migration within a given territory varies with the degree of diversity of areas included in that territory**. If positive and negative factors at the origin and destination are important in the migration process then significant socio-economic contrasts between the regions of a country should result in high levels of migration. High rates of internal migration in Mexico, Brazil, China and Egypt in recent decades exemplify such a situation.
2. **The volume of migration varies with the diversity of people**. Where differences among people are limited in terms of race, income, education, tradition and other variables, migration rates will be low, such as in present-day Scandinavia.
3. **The volume of migration is related to the difficulty of surmounting the intervening obstacles**. One of the most important considerations in the decision to migrate is the difficulty of getting from the origin to the destination. Illegal entry into the USA from the rest of the Americas is strongly related to the relative proximity of countries to the USA. It is not surprising that most illegal migrants come from Mexico.
4. **The volume of migration varies with fluctuations in the economy**. Regional differences usually widen during periods of economic expansion thus encouraging migration, while during periods of economic recession a levelling of opportunity tends to occur which reduces the urge to migrate. Britain in the twentieth century provides a good example of this hypothesis.
5. **Unless severe checks are imposed, both volume and rate of migration tend to increase with time**. This tends to happen for a number of reasons including the reduction of intervening obstacles, increasing national and international socio-economic contrasts and the increasing diversity of people. This was certainly the case in the USA in the nineteenth and early twentieth centuries before 'national origins quotas' were introduced in 1924.

6. **The volume and rate of migration vary with the state of progress in a country or area**. The rationale here is similar to that for the previous principle. Lee quotes the extremely high rates of internal migration within the USA and argues that in the least developed countries we should find a largely immobile population which usually changes residence only under duress, and then en masse rather than through individual action. It was the development of large scale economic activity in the emerging core region of LEDCs such as Egypt and Brazil which sparked high volume rural to urban migration.

(ii) Stream and counterstream

1. **Migration tends to take place largely within well defined streams**. Opportunities tend to be highly localised at specific destinations and migrants must usually follow established routes. Examples include the migration of Asians to Britain and British migration to Australia.
2. **For every major migration stream, a counterstream develops**. Counterstreams are established for a number of reasons. One contributory factor is that many migrants, for example those moving from Ireland to the USA and Britain, improve their status at the destination and may later be able to return to their origin on advantageous terms.
3. **The efficiency of the stream (ratio of stream to counterstream) is high if the major factors in the development of a migration stream are minus factors at the origin**. When the push factors at the origin are very severe the likelihood of migrants returning is minimal. The significant population movements caused by the break up of the former Soviet Union appear to be largely permanent. The ethnic conflicts which fuelled such migration makes return unlikely for the great majority.
4. **The efficiency of stream and counterstream tends to be low if origin and destination are similar.** In this case people moving in opposing flows move largely for the same reasons and tend to cancel each other out. Migration between Canada and the USA and between France and Germany are examples which fall into this category.
5. **The efficiency of migration streams will be high if the intervening obstacles are great**. When the journey is particularly difficult the likelihood of return will be low. The best examples of this are historical, such as the large scale emigration from Ireland during the potato famine in the mid-nineteenth century.
6. **The efficiency of a migration stream varies with economic conditions, being high in prosperous times and low in times of depression**. The pull of economic core regions is greater during economic booms but much reduced when an economy is in recession. Such a temporal pattern has been observed in most MEDCs and a number of LEDCs.

(iii) Characteristics of migrants

1. **Migration is selective**. Migrants are not a random sample at the origin but tend to be selective in terms of age, sex and economic status.
2. **Migrants responding primarily to plus factors at the destination tend to be positively selected.** Here there is no necessity to migrate but people of high economic status may do so for an even better quality of life.
3. **Migrants responding primarily to minus factors at the origin tend to be negatively selected**. When conditions at the origin are very difficult it is the most deprived who feel 'forced' to migrate.
4. **Taking all migrants together, selection tends to be bimodal**. For any given migration some migrants respond primarily to plus factors at the destination while others respond mainly to minus factors at the origin.
5. **The degree of positive selection increases with the difficulty of the intervening obstacles**. When the intervening obstacles are high it is only the strongest and the most adventurous who are likely to undertake the journey.
6. **The heightened propensity to migrate at certain stages of the life-cycle is important in the selection of migrants**. Events such as leaving the parental home and marriage happen at quite well defined ages. Life cycle migration has been well documented in a range of MEDCs, e.g. Canada, and LEDCs, e.g. China.
7. **The characteristics of migrants tends to be intermediate between the characteristics of the population at the origin and the population at the destination**. To move in the first place, most migrants tend to feel some affinity with their chosen destination. Once they arrive, this affinity will help them assimilate, to varying degrees, economically, socially, and politically. For example, migration to Australia from non-English speaking countries is dominated by those with some command of the English language.

g) A systems approach

Mabogunje, in his analysis of rural–urban migration in Africa, attempted to set the phenomenon in its economic and social context as part of a system of interrelated elements (Figure 5). The systems approach does not see migration in over-simplified terms of cause and effect, but as a circular, interdependent and self-modifying system.

In Mabogunje's framework, the African rural–urban migration system is operating in an environment of change. The system and the environment act and react with each other continuously. For example, expansion in the urban economy will stimulate migration from rural areas, while deteriorating economic conditions in the larger urban areas will result in a reduction of migration flows from rural areas.

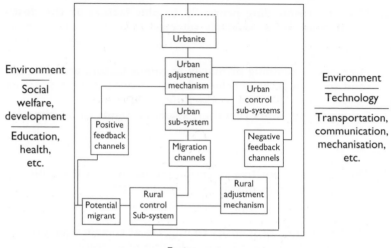

Figure 5 A systems approach to migration
(from A. Mabogunje (1970): Systems approach to a theory of rural–urban migration, Geographical Analysis 2:22)

If the potential migrant is stimulated to move to an urban area by the positive nature of the environment, he/she then comes under the influence of the 'rural control subsystem'. Here the attitudes of the potential migrant's family and local community come into play, either encouraging or restraining movement. If movement occurs, the migrant then comes under the influence of the 'urban control subsystem'. The latter will determine, by means of the employment and housing opportunities it offers, the degree to which migrants assimilate.

In addition there are adjustment mechanisms. For example, at the rural point of origin a positive adjustment resulting from out-migration might be increased income per head for the remaining villagers. The most likely negative adjustment will be the reduced level of social interaction between the out-migrants and their families. At the urban destination the in-migrant may benefit from the receipt of regular wages for the first time but as a result may be drawn into the negative aspects of lower income urban life such as gambling, excessive drinking and prostitution.

The flow of information between out-migrants and their rural origin is an important component of the system. Favourable reports from the new urban dwellers will generally increase the migration flow while negative perceptions will slow down the rate of movement.

4 Recent approaches to migration

Figure 6 summarises the main differences between the most recent approaches to migration, each of which is briefly discussed below.

a) The Todaro Model: the cost-benefit approach

In the post-1950 period there has been a huge movement of population from rural to urban areas in LEDCs. For many migrants it appeared that they had just swapped rural poverty for urban poverty. The simplistic explanation put forward was that many rural dwellers had been attracted by the 'bright lights' of the large urban areas without any clear understanding of the real deprivation of urban life for those at or near the bottom of the socio-economic scale. They had migrated due to false perceptions picked up from the media and other sources. The American economist Michael Todaro challenged this view arguing that migrants' perceptions of urban life were realistic, being strongly based on an accurate flow of information from earlier migrants from their rural community. Potential migrants carefully weighed up the costs and benefits of moving to urban areas including the 'anticipated income differential'. They were very aware that in the short term they might not be better off, but the likelihood was that their socio-economic standing would improve in the long term. Thus, people were

Determinants of migration	Effects	Unit of analysis		
		Individual	Household/family	Institutions
Economic	Positive	Todaro Push-pull	Stark and others; 'new economics' of migration	
	Negative			Marxism Structuralism
Sociological/ anthropological		◄———— Structuration theory ————► ◄———— Gender analyses ————►		

Figure 6 Recent approaches to migration studies
Source: The Journal of Development Studies, Vol 36, No 2, December 1999

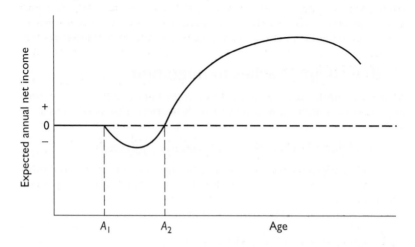

Figure 7 A typical net-income stream
Source: Population: An Introduction by J. Overbeck

willing to endure short term difficulties in the hope of better prospects eventually, if not for themselves then for their children.

Figure 7 summarises the typical net-income stream of a young rural to urban migrant. While at school the young rural dweller's net income is zero. At A1 he migrates to a large urban area but is initially unable to find work because of the intense competition for employment and the limited nature of his contacts. His net income is negative as he has no option but to live on savings or borrowed money. However, in time, as his knowledge of the city improves and his contact base widens, he finds employment and his net income becomes positive (A2), rising to a peak and then decreasing with age as his productivity begins to fall.

b) Stark's 'New Economics of Migration'

Stark, in what is often referred to as the 'New Economics of Migration' has extended the Todaro Model by replacing the individual with the household as the unit of analysis. Stark, along with others, argued that insufficient attention had been paid to the institutions that determine migration. For example, in the Todaro Model it is assumed that migrants act individually according to a rationality of economic self-interest. However, migration according to Stark, is seen as a form of economic diversification by families whereby the costs and rewards are shared. It is a form of risk spreading. Stark asserts that 'even though the entities that engage in migration are often individual agents, there is more to labour migration than an individualistic optimising behaviour.'

Often the initial cost of establishing the rural migrant in an urban area is carried by the family in the expectation of returns in the form of remittances. The migrant also has expectations in maintaining the link, for example by way of inheritance. A number of studies have described how families invest in the education of one member of the family, usually the firstborn son, for migration to the urban formal sector. The expectation is that the remittances received will be crucial to the up-bringing of the remaining children and have an important effect on the general standard of living of the family.

c) Marxist/Structuralist Theory

Some writers, often in the tradition of Marxist analyses, see labour migration as inevitable in the transition to capitalism. Migration is the only option for survival after alienation from the land. Structuralist theory draws attention to the advantages of migrant labour for capitalist production and emphasises the control that capitalism has over migrant labour. For example employers use migrant labour to reduce the bargaining power of local labour. In the international arena, migration is seen as a global movement in which labour is manipulated in the interest of MEDCs to the detriment of LEDCs. According to Rubenstein, remittances are 'a minor component of surplus labour extraction, a small charge to capital in a grossly unequal process of exchange between core and peripheral societies'.

d) Structuration Theory

Structuration Theory, as developed by Anthony Giddens, incorporates both individual motives for migration and the structural factors in which the migrants operate. It stresses that rules designed to regulate behaviour also provide opportunity and room for manoeuvre for those they seek to constrain. This approach also builds in an awareness of cultural factors.

c) Gender analyses

In recent decades gender has come to occupy a significant place in migration literature. According to de Haan 'There is now much more emphasis on the different migration responses by men and women, which themselves are context dependent, and on gender discrimination in returns to migrant labour'.

5 Migration data

There are three principal sources of migration data; censuses, population registers and social surveys. For all three, moves are recorded as migration when an official boundary used for data collection is crossed. Moves which do not cross a boundary may go unrecorded even though they may cover longer distances. This is one of the major problems encountered by the researcher in the study of migration.

Population censuses are important sources of information because they are taken at regular intervals and cover whole countries. The two sorts of data generally provided are birthplaces of the population and period migration figures (movement over a particular period of time). Birthplace data tell us a great deal about the broad picture of migration but they are not without their deficiencies. For example, there is no information about the number of residential moves between place of birth and present residence. In terms of period migration, recent British censuses have asked for place of residence one year before the census as well as place of birth. When these are compared with the present addresses of people at the time of the census we can begin to trace migration patterns. However, intervening moves during the one year period and between censuses (every ten years in Britain) will go unrecorded. Nevertheless it was these census sources which Ravenstein used to formulate his 'Laws of Migration'.

The first census of England and Wales was in 1801. Over the years the format of the census has changed considerably. Preparation for the census in 2001 began as early as 1993. Various tests were conducted particularly with regard to new and revised questions. It is important that all questions are clear and allow people to respond with accuracy. The census provides a benchmark for official population estimates. Between censuses the population figures are rolled forward using annual estimates of the components of population change. As the decade proceeds, problems with estimating migration, in particular, progressively affect these rolled-forward figures. A new census is used for both revising previous years' data and for providing a base for the estimates in the following decade.

Japan and a number of European countries (including Norway, Sweden and Switzerland) collect 'continuous data' on migration through *population registers*. Inhabitants are required to register an address with the police or a civic authority and to notify all changes of residence. Population registers aim to record every move, rather than just those caught by the rather arbitrary framework of the census. In Britain and many other countries only partial registers exist to record movements for some parts of the population. Examples are electoral rolls, tax registers and school rolls. Social researchers have argued for the introduction of population registers in countries like Britain but strong opposition has focused on possible infringements of civil liberties. Thus, it was only under the exceptional circumstances of World War Two and its immediate aftermath that a national register operated in Britain.

Specific surveys can do much to supplement the sources of data discussed above. An example from Britain is the International Passenger Survey, a sample survey carried out at seaports and airports. It was established to provide information on tourism and the effect of travel expenditure on the balance of payments, but it also provides useful information on international migration. The annual General Household Survey of 15,000 households also provides useful information as does the biennial Labour Force Survey. Questionnaire-based surveys are perhaps the only means by which the relationship between attitudes and behaviour in the migration process can be fully analysed.

Even when all the available sources of information are used to analyse migration patterns, the investigator can be left in no doubt that a large proportion of population movements go entirely unrecorded. Even in those countries with the most advanced administrative systems there is only partial recording of migrants and their characteristics.

Summary

- Migration is defined as a 'permanent' change of residence lasting more than one year.
- Migration typologies are classifications of migrations into types. The main elements of classification are distance, duration and cause.
- The concept of the Mobility Transition encompasses the full range of human movement, differentiating particularly between circulation and migration.
- Ravenstein's Laws of Migration, based on census data for the late nineteenth century, provided the basis for much of the theoretical work that was to follow.
- The Inverse Distance Law and the Gravity Model introduced mathematical formulae to migration research.
- Stouffer's Theory of Intervening Opportunities was an important conceptual development.
- Lee's Principles of Migration attempted to bring together all aspects of migration theory to date.
- Mabogunje adopted a systems approach to explain rural–urban migration in Africa.
- The Todaro Model takes a cost-benefit approach to rural–urban migration, opposing the simplistic 'bright lights' explanation.
- Stark's 'New Economics of Migration' replaces the individual as the unit of analysis (Todaro) with the household.
- The three main sources of migration data are population censuses, population registers and social surveys.

Questions

1. Study Figure 2.
   a With reference to an example, explain what is meant by 'primitive' migration.
   b What is the difference between 'forced' and 'impelled' migration?
   c Explain the distinction between conservative migration and innovating migration.
   d Examine the causes of a mass migration you have studied.
2. Study Figure 3.
   a Define the terms 'mobility' and 'circulation'.
   b Describe and explain the changes between Phases I and II of the Mobility Transition.
   c Account for the changes in (i) international migration and (ii) rural to urban migration over the five phases of the Mobility Transition.
3. Study Figure 4.
   a Define the terms (i) origin (ii) destination (iii) intervening obstacles.
   b Why does the nature of positive and negative factors often vary from one person to another?
   c How have the intervening obstacles between origin and destination changed over time?
   d With reference to a long term migration between countries or regions, assess the importance of major positive and negative factors at origin and destination.
4. Study Figure 5.
   a What do you understand by a 'systems approach' to migration?
   b Suggest how the 'rural control sub-system' might affect a potential migration decision.
   c Outline three ways in which the urban sub-system can impact on rural–urban migration.
   d Explain the influence of positive and negative feedback channels on new potential migrants.

3 A brief history of migration

1 Introducton

Humankind has been migrating for millions of years. This continuous process has affected all parts of the world to varying degrees and for different time periods. Any attempt to condense such an important aspect of human history in a short chapter invariably demands selectivity and risks unmerited omission. Thus, the aim of what follows is simply to give the student a flavour of some of the most important movements that have occurred over time.

2 The diffusion of early humankind

The first hominids, Australopithecus, appeared in Africa between four and five million years ago, on a planet which is generally accepted to be 4,600 million years old. They differed from their predecessors, the apes, as they walked on two legs and did not use their hands for weight-bearing. After two million years cranial capacity had increased by 50% from the 600 cm^3 of the earliest hominid, Australopithecus, to the 900 cm^3 of the primitive human named Homo erectus. The final increase to Homo sapiens' average brain size of 1450 cm^3 took place about 100,000 years ago.

The evolution of humankind was matched by its geographical diffusion in the search for new opportunities. Whereas the locational evidence for Australopithecus is confined to Africa, remains of Homo erectus have been found stretching from Europe to south east Asia. Homo sapiens roamed even further, making the first incursions into the cold environments of high latitudes. When the ice retreated at the end of the last Ice Age, bands of hunters followed herds of mammoths right into the Arctic Circle.

Early humans survived by hunting and gathering, moving continuously in search of food supplies. Their intellectual superiority over

The 10 families of man who settled Europe are revealed in gene tests

BY ROGER HIGHFIELD
SCIENCE EDITOR

EUROPEAN men are almost all related to just 10 male lineages whose descendants migrated from the east in three waves over the past 40,000 years, scientists report today.

A genetic study of 1,007 men across Europe and the Middle East found that 95 per cent of them could be traced to one of 10 categories.

On average, more than 80 per cent of European men have inherited characteristics from two waves of Palaeolithic ancestors 40,000 and 25,000 years ago, according to the study published in the journal *Science*.

The oldest male lineage – characterised by a genetic marker called M173 – contributes to half of the genetic make-up of European males.

Their advent coincides with the arrival of what archaeologists call the Aurignacian people, known for rock art and finely crafted tools.

The second wave is thought to be called the Gravettian culture, known for its Venus figurines and delicate blades. The remainder were thought to have arrived after an ice age some 10,000 years ago, when there was a third – Neolithic – migration of the first farmers from the Fertile Crescent in the Middle East.

The higher levels of the latter genetic make up in the south of Europe suggest that some of these farmers travelled by boat along the coast.

The international team, led by Dr Ornella Semino, from Pavia University in Italy, studied the "male" chromosome – Y chromosomes – of men. Since its genetic information passes only from father to son, DNA variations on the Y chromosome can be used to trace paternal ancestry. The researchers analysed 22 such markers, and found that nearly all the individuals in the study could be linked to 10 groups of male ancestors.

The investigators said: "Two lineages … appear to have been present in Europe since Palaeolithic times.

"The remaining lineages entered Europe most likely later during independent migrations from the Middle East and the Urals."

Figure 8 European descendants
Source: Daily Telegraph 10/11/2000

previously dominant species allowed them to spread much further than their predecessors. Racial differences arose in response to the need to survive in strongly contrasting geographical environments. The spread of human population was absolutely essential for its increase in numbers.

Migration out of Africa was first to Asia and then from Asia to Europe (Figure 8). In Asia humankind found the grassy steppes a particularly attractive environment. However, this did not inhibit movement further afield. For example, the majority of the peoples of South East Asia are descended from the Mongol pastoral nomads of central Asia. Neanderthal man populated Europe during the last Ice Age, but was supplanted or absorbed about 40,000 years ago by Homo sapiens. Because of ice cover Scandinavia was the last part of Europe to be inhabited, perhaps by about 10,000 BC.

Oceania and the Americas

The last of the habitable continents to be peopled were Oceania and the Americas.

Around 70,000 BC the Indonesian islands were inhabited by ancestors of the present-day Melanesians. At that time Oceania was uninhabited. During a major glacial period sea level fell by 100 metres, resulting in the appearance of new islands that had previously been submerged, linking up at many points along the archipelago. This provided a route for the Melanesians to reach first New Guinea and then Australia, the latter by about 50,000 BC. This was the beginning of the peopling of Oceania. By 5000 BC when the last Ice Age was over, the population of Australia-New Guinea is estimated to have reached 250,000. However, it was not until the second millennium BC that the islands to the east of New Guinea were discovered and colonised. The Tonga Islands were populated from 1000 BC and the Samoan Islands from 300 BC. By the beginning of the Christian era these outliers of the Melanesian world were sufficiently different from it in culture and language to merit the separate title of Polynesia. Between the fourth and tenth centuries AD the seafaring skills of the Polynesians took them to Tahiti, Hawaii, the Cook Islands and New Zealand.

The first colonists entered North America from Siberia during the last or 'Wisconsin' glaciation when the formation of ice sheets locked up so much water on the land that sea levels were lowered by as much as 100 metres and the shallow sea bed of the Bering Strait emerged as dry land. As mammoths, steppe bison and horses crossed the land bridge, their hunters followed, perhaps as early as 25,000 BC. Gradually these groups and their descendents spread throughout North, central and South America. The initial movement from Alaska to lands further south followed two routes. It appears that most of these early migrants took a land route along the ice-free corridor between the Laurentian ice sheet (Arctic islands and Canadian

Shield) and the Cordilleran ice sheet (Rocky Mountains). Smaller groups travelled by sea from southern Alaska, landing just south of the Cordilleran ice sheet in the present-day state of Washington.

From the time of the first movement of people across the Bering Strait, it took about 15,000 years for groups to spread throughout South America. Stone artefacts found at Fell's Cave in Patagonia reveal that people had reached the southernmost tip of South America by 10,000 BC. South America, like North America, offered vast areas where hunting and gathering were very productive. The Inuit (eskimos) who inhabit the northernmost lands in the Americas were relative latecomers in the great migrations from eastern Asia. It is thought that they crossed into North America about 4000 BC, gradually spreading to the east. The Inuit eventually reached Greenland about 2500 BC.

By AD 1 the area now covered by the USA and Canada had a population of about 300,000 people. This increased to 500,000 by AD 1000. The first Europeans to reach North America were the Norse people who landed on the Labrador coast at about this time. They were few in number and it is thought that their community was abandoned after just a few generations. Between AD 1000 and AD 1500 the population of North America doubled and diffused more widely over the continental area. However, from about AD 1500 onwards the continent was influenced by a new and powerful source; sustained migration, mainly from Europe.

3 The development of empires

As humankind spread beyond its African origins, mortality rates declined and population increased. However, such growth was extremely slow compared with the rates of increase experienced in recent centuries. Nevertheless, the absolute increase in population that occurred over thousands of years proved to be the calalyst for the transition from migratory hunting and gathering to migratory slash and burn agriculture. There followed a rapid diffusion of crop growing with barley and wheat, moving west and east from the Middle East across the whole of Eurasia within about 5000 years. It has been estimated that 10,000 years ago, when sedentary agriculture first developed, world population was no more than 5 million. Known as the Neolithic Revolution, this period of economic change, based on a more substantial and securer food source, significantly altered the relationship between people and their environments.

The next pulse of migration began around 4000 to 3000 BC, stimulated by the development of seagoing sailing boats and by pastoral nomadry. The centre of maritime culture at this time was the Mediterranean Sea with other active areas being the Indian Ocean and the South China Sea. The dual thrust in all these regions was deep sea fishing and trade over longer distances than had been experienced before. The seafarers colonised uninhabited lands and imposed their rule by force over less mobile populations. The pastoralists spread across the expansive grasslands of the Eurasian Steppe and the African and Middle Eastern savannas, gaining military advantage over the sedentary farmers they came into contact with due to their superior mobility and nutrition. Even as agricultural advance continued, pastoral nomadry persisted, providing important networks for the diffusion of new technology.

The development of the first cities, around 3500 BC, in the valleys of the Tigris and Euphrates rivers, was a fundamentally important stage in the spread of people and the diffusion of ideas. Compared with anything that had gone before, these new settlements were distinctive in size, function and appearance. However, the basis of the earliest urban centres was relatively local. For example, the population of Sumerian cities ranged from 7000 to 20 000. This first 'urban revolution' fostered political differentiation into ruling classes and ruled masses, providing a basis for the imposition of taxes and rents that financed the development of professional soldiers and artisans. Military and economic superiority allowed these advanced communities to expand by direct conquest. Thus, migration patterns played a significant role in creating early empires and cultures.

Figure 9 A relic of the Roman Empire in North Africa.

Considerably later than the first cities, trading centres began to develop. The Minoan civilisation cities of Knossos and Phaistos which flourished in Crete during the first half of the second millennium BC derived their wealth from maritime trade. The Greeks and then the Romans developed urban and trading systems on a scale larger than ever before. These were times of considerable human movement. As one population conquered or infiltrated another, the vanquished were usually destroyed, enslaved or forcibly absorbed. Large numbers of people were captured and transported by slave traders. Major examples include the Dorian incursions in ancient Greece in the eleventh century BC and the Germanic migrations southward from the Baltic to the Roman Empire in the fourth to sixth centuries AD. Later examples include the Norman raids and conquests of Britain between the eighth and twelfth centuries AD and the Bantu migrations in Africa throughout the Christian era.

4 Global migrations

a) The Americas: European colonisation

In 1492 Christopher Columbus landed in the West Indies. This was the beginning of the modern age of settlement in the Americas. Soon other explorers sailed west to the New World, among them Amerigo Vespucci whose name was used to describe the new lands. Apart from a few thousand British convicts sentenced to 'transportation' in the seventeenth and eighteenth centuries, the movement of European settlers to the Americas was completely voluntary.

The earliest large scale European migrants to the Americas in the sixteenth century were the Spanish and Portuguese with 100,000 Spanish settling in the Spanish-American Empire and 10,000 Portuguese opting for Brazil. It was not until the seventeenth century that the lure of the Americas spread to northern Europe. By 1700 there were 0.3 million people of European origin in North America compared to 1 million in Latin America. It has been estimated that the net trans-Atlantic movement between 1492 and 1700 was under 0.5 million. The figures for the eighteenth century were not that much different with 0.4 million migrants going to North America and 0.2 million to Latin America. It was not until well into the nineteenth century that the scale of migration really began to change. The 'Great Migration' of 1845 to 1914 brought 41 million people to the Americas with the vast majority (35 million) landing in North America. This had a dramatic impact on the ethnic structure of the Americas as Europeans became the dominant group at the expense of Amerindians and Afro-Americans.

Africans were brought to the Americas as slaves, in what was the largest forced migration in history. The slave trade developed out of Portugal's fifteenth century interest in African exploration. At first the Portuguese used slaves on their sugar plantations in Madeira and the Azores. But when Brazil was found to be an even better place for cultivating sugar, the trans-Atlantic slave trade commenced. After about 1650 the slave trade ceased to be purely Portuguese, when the British, French and Dutch began to import African slaves on a large scale, mainly into the Caribbean. By the end of the seventeenth century the Caribbean population numbered about 300,000 African slaves and 200,000 Europeans. By 1850 the total number of slaves brought into the Caribbean was 4 million. After the Caribbean the biggest market for slaves was Brazil where 3.5 million were landed by the mid nineteenth century. The Black population of North America was first established when 20 young slaves were taken to Virginia in 1619. However, in total only 0.4 million African slaves were landed in North America and the use of slaves never really spread outside the southern states of the USA.

In North America the Spanish explored much of the south and west of what is now the USA. Settlement was limited but missionaries did establish the sites of some of today's large cities, including San Francisco (1775) and Los Angeles (1781). French exploration was centred around the St Lawrence river, the Great Lakes and the Mississippi river as far south as New Orleans. The fur trade was the basis of the French presence. The first permanent English settlement was established in 1607 at Jamestown, Virginia. Soon many more settlements developed on, and inland from, the Atlantic coastline. Along the east coast, colonies were established under the control of England although people were also arriving from many other European countries.

As settlement spread inland, a series of conflicts arose with the Indians, the French and the Spanish. As the eighteenth century progressed, relations between the 13 colonies and Britain became strained. The worsening relationship led to the War of Independence (1776–83). Under the Peace Treaty of 1783, Britain recognised the independence of the 13 states, agreeing that the new nation should have all the land east of the Mississippi. In the next century the USA was to expand even more as the frontier (the area settled by people of European origin) moved towards the Pacific Ocean (Figure 10).

Before European settlement, a considerable proportion of the Indian population lived in the eastern part of what was to become the USA. As the frontier pushed forward the Indians were removed from these lands and forced to live on reservations, most of which were on poor quality land in the West. Perhaps the most notorious of these forced migrations occurred in 1838 when the last remaining Indians of the south east nations (Creeks, Cherokees, Choctaws, Chickasaws) were forced off their land and directed to land prepared for them to the west of the Mississippi River. A quarter of this migrant population perished on the winter journey which became known as the 'Trail of Tears'. Of the almost one billion hectares that native Americans roamed 500 years ago, less than 19 million remain in Indian hands today.

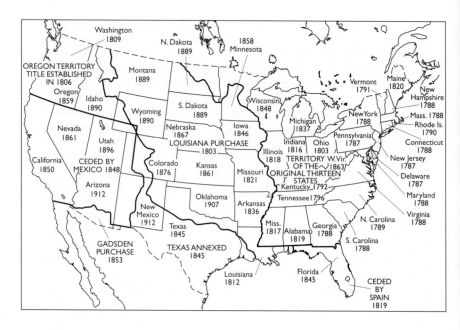

Figure 10 Territorial expansion of the USA
Source: North America in Focus, P. Guinness, Hodder & Stoughton, 1990

The South is the historic nucleus of the black population in the USA. However, from 1910 many blacks left farming for work in the cities, partly because their small farms could not compete with the large mechanised farms of the white landowners. They migrated in large numbers to the rapidly growing industrial cities of the north east and mid-west in one of the great migration streams of US history.

The population of the USA has continued to spread to the West and the South. For example, in 1960 California took over from New York as the most highly populated state in the USA. Since then the gap has widened considerably. In the USA people use the term 'sunbelt' to refer to the southern part of the country from Florida to California. For decades this has been a region of generally strong economic growth. In contrast the 'frostbelt' states of the north east and mid-west have seen many of their traditional industries decline.

While in North America the migration of those of European origin was generally from East to West, in South America it was inland from ports established on both the Atlantic and Pacific coasts. The cultivation of sugar dominated the economy of coastal Brazil in the early years of Portuguese settlement, while mineral resources and potential farmland were the opportunities sought by those who ventured inland. The most important consequence of early expeditions into the interior was the discovery of gold, first found in 1695 in Minas Gerais. In 1719 gold was also discovered in Mato Grosso, adding fresh impetus to the opening up of the interior. Possibly as many as 800,000 Portuguese arrived in Brazil in the 100 years following the first discovery of gold. By the 1730s the search for gold had reached into the Amazon basin. Unfortunately the gold boom did not last and the economic outlook for Brazil at the end of the colonial period was not good. However, the nineteenth century was to bring more speculative 'booms', attracting further large scale immigration.

Significant movement into the interior had to await the construction of railroads and roads, and a government that made the development of the interior a national priority. The latter was indeed a key policy element under the presidency of Juscelino Kubitschek (1956–61). Kubitschek was the founder of Brasilia which became the new capital city when the government moved from Rio de Janeiro in 1960. Located almost 1000 km from the Atlantic coast, Brasilia was seen as an essential catalyst for the development of the interior. The second key element of the strategy to develop the interior was to encourage migration into the Amazon region. Not only would this help to integrate the Amazon region into the national economy but it would also ease the migration pressure on the rapidly growing cities of the south east region.

Elsewhere in South America the pattern of internal migration has been broadly similar. Governments have been anxious to develop peripheral regions but have found it difficult to stem the tide of migration from rural peripheral regions to urban core regions.

5 million people left Europe for various destinations between the voyages of discovery and the year 1845; ten times that number left between 1845 and the outbreak of the First World War. The British Isles and Russia contributed over 10 million people each in these mass migrations. Germany, Italy and Austro-Hungary added 5 million each, and Scandinavia contributed 2.5 million. The USA, which attracted 30 million new citizens was the most popular destination, but Canada, South America, Australia and (in the Russian case) Siberia received a large volume of new settlers too. Movement on this huge scale was facilitated by the steamship and the railway, and was encouraged by the promise of greater opportunity in the newly settled lands.

b) Russian migration to Siberia

In Asia, the Great Siberian Migration is of particular note. The first Russians crossed the Urals at the end of the sixteenth century. They established control over the whole area at an astonishing speed and by 1700 the Russian flag was flying on the Sea of Okhotsk and 100,000 Russian fur trappers and traders had been added to the 200,000 native hunters and fishers. Russian peasants, prisoners and political exiles followed and by 1800 the total population had risen to 1 million, rising further to 2.5 million by 1850. By the mid nineteenth century the peasant masses of European Russia had become aware of the opportunities that existed in the East, commencing one of the great migrations in history. The number of new colonists arriving each year passed the 25,000 mark in 1870, reaching 50,000 a year in 1890 and 100,000 in 1896, the year the first major section of the Trans-Siberian railway was opened. In the period 1901–14 an average of 200,000 Russians migrated annually to Siberia. By 1914 the total population of Siberia had reached 14 million and the cumulative total of immigrants was nearing 7 million. Although migration flows never reached this rate thereafter, Siberia remained an important destination for Russian migrants with the total population reaching 27 million in 1950, 34 million in 1975, with an estimate of almost 40 million for 2000.

c) South Africa

Of all the population movements which have occurred in Africa perhaps none have left a more problematic legacy than migration into South Africa. By the first millenium AD the southern and central parts of the country were inhabited by Khoikhoi (Hottentots) and small bands of San (Bushmen). By about 1500 Bantu-speaking black Africans from east-central Africa had reached the region. In 1488 Bartolomeu Dias, a Portuguese navigator, became the first European to round the Cape of Good Hope, although the first permanent European settlement was not established until 1652 when a provisioning station for the Dutch East India Company was set up by Jan van Riebeeck. Soon van Riebeeck established trade with nearby Khoikhoi and brought in as slaves black Africans from western and eastern Africa as well as Malayans from south east Asia. Gradually the Europeans moved inland, as most San and Khoihoi migrated into inaccessible parts of the country to avoid European domination.

During the eighteenth century interbreeding between Khoikhoi, slaves and Europeans began to create what later became known as the coloured population. At this time white farmers (the Boers) moved further inland. By 1750 they encountered the Xhosa (a Bantu people) and in 1779 the first of a long series of so-called Kaffir Wars broke out. In 1814 the Cape territory was assigned to Britain by the Congress of Vienna. The Boers (of Dutch descent) were disaffected by British rule and about 12,000 of them left the Cape between 1835 and 1843 in what is known as the Great Trek. In the 1850s the Boer republics of the Orange Free State and the Transvaal were established.

In 1860 the first indentured labourers from India arrived in Natal to work on the sugar plantations and by 1900 they outnumbered the whites there. Increasing tensions between the British and the Boers led the Transvaal and the Orange Free State to declare war on Britain in 1899. The Boer War, won by the British, ended in 1902. In the post-Second World War period the Afrikaner-oriented Nationalist Party dominated South African politics and greatly strengthened white control of the country. The policy of segregating whites and non-whites (apartheid) was implemented by laws that included curbs on free movement and the establishment of a number of 'independent' homelands for black Africans.

While South Africa came under fierce international criticism for its overtly racist policies, the extremely high standard of living enjoyed by whites attracted considerable white immigration into the country. However, since the end of White Rule in 1994 a significant number of whites have left the country, in a phenomenon which has been called the 'white flight', due to rising unemployment among that section of the population, a huge increase in the crime rate and general uncertainty about the future prospects of the country.

d) Oceania: European colonisation

The European colonisation of Oceania began in January 1788 when a fleet of British ships disembarked about a thousand people at Port Jackson, near present-day Sydney. As in the Americas the native population succumbed quickly to the new diseases brought in by the Europeans. In Australia, New Zealand and Hawaii, the worst affected land masses in the region, the native population fell from 700,000 in 1800 to 150,000 in 1900. The fall in native population was considerably less in the other islands of the region which were of much less interest to the European colonisers. Between 1788 and 1867, 150,000 British convicts were transported to Australia. From 0.6 million in 1850 Australia's population increased rapidly to 19 million in 2000. Over the same period New Zealand's population grew from 0.1 million to 3.8 million. In both cases continued immigration has been a major contributor to population increase. Both Australia and New Zealand were significant destinations for refugees, mostly European, after the Second World War. In the 25 years after 1945, over 350,000 refugees settled in Australia with some 7000 going to New Zealand.

By the mid-1970s Britain had supplied 75% of all migrants to Australia and 90% of those settling in New Zealand. Although the influence of this source area is still dominant, other European countries such as Italy and Greece have figured more prominently as areas of origin in recent decades, as have a number of Asian nations. Although Australia only ended its 'White Australia' immigration policy in 1973, from 1975 the country accepted the largest number of Indochinese refugees for resettlement after the USA and Canada. This amounted to over 185,000 people. Of particular sociological interest in the rest of the region are the French who settled in New Caledonia, the Indians who came as indentured labourers to Fiji, and the Japanese, Chinese, Filipino and American melting pot in Hawaii.

e) The First and Second World Wars

The First World War led to a movement of nearly 8 million people with numerous smaller-scale movements following cessation of hostilities. These included people fleeing from the Spanish Civil War, the establishment of Facism in Italy and the anti-Jewish policies in Germany in the 1930s. The Second World War provoked a massive displacement of people, some permanently, some temporarily. Many of these movements have proved difficult to quantify, but one estimate is that 25 million people moved during and immediately after the Second World War. The Nazi government of Germany deported 7–8 million people, including 5 million Jews later exterminated in concentration camps. After the Second World War, 9–10 million ethnic Germans were more or less forcibly transported into Germany, and an estimated one million members of minority groups deemed politically unreliable by the Soviet government were forcibly exiled to central Asia.

f) The Partition of India

In 1947 British India was partitioned to form the separate nations of Hindu dominated India and Muslim dominated Pakistan. This decision left large minorities of Hindus and Sikhs in Pakistan, and Muslims in India. The tensions between the two main communities erupted in widespread violence in late 1947 in which more than 500,000 people died. In fear of their lives 7.5 million Muslim refugees fled to both parts of Pakistan (East and West) from India while 10 million Hindus left Pakistan for India. However, this was not to be the end of mass movement in the Indian sub-continent. In 1971 civil war erupted in Pakistan when East Pakistan (Bangladesh) proclaimed its independence from the more powerful West Pakistan. During the months of conflict an estimated one million Bengalis were killed in East Pakistan and another 10 million fled into exile in India.

g) Afghanistan

Afghan refugees began fleeing their country in 1979 following invasion by the Soviet Union. They remain the largest group dealt with by United Nations High Commissioner for Refugess (UNHCR) with 1.4 million resettled in Iraq and 820,000 in Pakistan, despite the fact that 3.89 million people have returned to Afghanistan since the beginning of the exodus, following Soviet withdrawal. When the fundamentalist Taliban came to power after Soviet withdrawal they imposed Islamic law in Kabul. As a result a fresh round of population displacements began both within Afghanistan and to Pakistan.

h) Northwest Europe: guestworkers and asylum seekers

Large scale immigration into western Europe is a relatively recent phenomenon. In post-war Europe a number of countries could not satisfy the domestic demand for labour from their own populations, and looked to less prosperous parts of Europe, nearby countries outside of the continent and former colonies to make up the shortfall. However, with the onset of the energy crisis in 1973 attitudes to immigration changed with European governments making it more difficult for immigrants to get in. However, Europe, and the most affluent EU countries in particular, is the desired destination of a huge number of economic migrants and refugees. Refugees from other continents first began arriving in Europe in large numbers during the 1970s. They included refugees fleeing from Latin America as a result of the military coups in Chile and Uruguay in 1973 and Argentina in 1976. Although the majority of refugees fleeing Indochina after 1975 were resettled in North America, some 230,000 were taken in by Western Europe.

In the mid-1980s the number of asylum seekers began to cause serious concern. The increase from under 70,000 in 1983 to over 200,000 in 1989 was linked to the number of internal conflicts and serious human rights violations in Asia, Africa and the Middle East, and Latin America. Asylum applications hit a peak of almost 700,000 in 1992. In the late 1990s labour shortages, particularly in the information technology field, again became apparent in a number of EU countries leading to a relaxation of restrictions for those with coveted skills.

i) The collapse of the Soviet Union and Yugoslavia

A United Nations report published in 1996 concluded that more than 9 million former Soviet citizens had migrated across the new international borders created by the disintegration of the Soviet Union. Ethnic disputes in Georgia, Armenia and Azerbaijan resulted in 1.5 million people leaving their homelands. Similar population movements resulted from fighting in Moldova, Tajikistan and Chechnia. The Russian Federation has absorbed the biggest inflow of people as ethnic Russians have sought the safety of their motherland. In the Soviet era, Russians moved to other republics where they were put in positions of authority. As Russian was the accepted language of the Soviet Union few ethnic Russians made the effort to learn the local language. Now the latter is usually a job requirement as the new nations assert their freedom from Russian rule.

The former Soviet states are also trying to unravel Stalin's migration policy which involved moving 3 million people from their homes to other Soviet regions. Large national groups such as Volga Germans, Chechens and Crimea Tatars were moved in cattle trucks to Siberia or central Asia. Many of their descendants now want to return home. When the Soviet system collapsed, many observers feared a wave of immigration from this region to the West. In fact most of the population movements have been contained within the borders of the former Soviet Union.

The term 'ethnic cleansing' has come to be synonymous with the disintegration of Yugoslavia in the 1990s, giving Europe its largest refugee problem in the post-war period. The crisis in the former Yugoslavia created 4 million refugees and displaced people, the largest population movement in Europe since the end of the Second World War.

j) The Great Lakes region of Africa

While the ethnic problems of the Great Lakes region have a long and complex history, international attention began to focus on Rwanda in mid-1994 when at least 500,000 people, mostly Tutsis, were killed by Hutus in the space of six weeks. As the tables turned the organisers of the genocide recognised their imminent defeat and organised a mass evacuation of the Hutu population. 1.75 million people fled from Rwanda to Tanzania, DR Congo (formerly Zaire) and Burundi. However, a similar ethnic conflict was occurring in the latter country resulting in 160,000 Burundians fleeing to DR Congo and Tanzania. Most of the refugees from both countries eventually returned to their home regions.

5 Rural to urban migration: a global phenomenon

All countries at some stage over the last two centuries have experienced the phenomenon of rural to urban migration. In MEDCs urbanisation and industrialisation went hand in hand. As Britain was the first country to undergo the Industrial Revolution it was also the first to experience the associated urbanisation. This began in the latter half of the eighteenth century. By 1801 nearly one-tenth of the population of England and Wales was living in cities of over 100,000 people. This proportion doubled in 40 years and doubled again in another 60 years. As the processes of the Industrial Revolution spread to other countries, the pace of urbanisation quickened. The change from a population of 10% to 30% living in urban areas of over 100,000 people took 80 years in England and Wales; 66 years in the USA; 48 years in Germany; 36 years in Japan and 26 years in Australia.

The urbanisation of LEDCs has occurred largely since 1950. Because urban areas in the developing world have been growing much more quickly than the cities of the developed world did in the nineteenth century the term 'urban explosion' has been used to describe contemporary trends. Between 1990 and 1995, the world's urban population grew by nearly 60 million, with four-fifths of this increase in the LEDCs.

Counterurbanisation

Urban deconcentration is the most consistent and dominant feature of population movement in most MEDCs at present. Each level of the settlement hierarchy is gaining people from the more urban tiers above it but losing population to those below it. The signs of counterurbanisation are just beginning to appear in some of the most affluent of the LEDCs.

Summary

- The first hominids appeared in Africa about 5 million years ago.
- The subsequent evolution of humankind was matched by its geographical diffusion, first to Asia and then to Europe.
- Oceania and the Americas were the last continents to be inhabited.
- Technological development stimulated further movement, first within and then between continents.
- The European discovery of the Americas was the precursor to one of the great migrations in human history.
- People of European origin came to dominate Australia and New Zealand in a similar fashion to the Americas. However, in areas where native populations were much larger, the independence of the indigenous population was the inevitable outcome.
- A number of significant migration streams have occurred within the USA, most notably the forced migration of American Indians to reservations much further west than their historic tribal areas, the movement of black Americans from the agricultural South to the industrial North in the early part of the twentieth century, and the continuous population shift towards the West and the South.
- In recent years the fragmentation of national entities, for example the Soviet Union and Yugoslavia, has resulted in considerable population movement.
- Rural to urban migration has affected all countries to varying degrees. Its time span in MEDCs was from the late eighteenth century to the first half of the twentieth century. In LEDCs it has occurred largely since 1950.
- Counterurbanisation is a phenomenon as yet largely restricted to MEDCs.

Questions

1. Study Figure 8 and the first section of this chapter.
   a Describe the geographical diffusion of early humankind.
   b Suggest why migration out of Africa was initially to Asia and then to Europe as opposed to the other continents.
   c Why was Scandinavia the last part of Europe to be inhabited?
   d Evaluate the evidence presented in Figure 8 concerning the ancestry of Europeans.
2. Study Figure 10 and the text relating to the peopling of the Americas.
   a Describe the peopling of the Americas before European colonisation.
   b Why were the Americas initially colonised from Asia as opposed to Europe?
   c What does Figure 10 tell you about the diffusion of settlement in the USA in recent centuries?
   d Comment on the major migrations in the USA since European colonisation.

4 Internal migration in LEDCs

1 Classifying population movements

a) The spatial perspective

Figure 11 provides a comprehensive classification of population movements in LEDCs covering distance, direction and pattern. The 'distance continuum' ranges from relatively limited local movements to very long distance movements, often crossing international frontiers. However, it must be remembered that thousands of people in LEDCs who live close to international borders may migrate relatively short distances into another country to find employment.

As Parnwell (1993) states 'Distance provides a useful basis for differentiating between types of movement and types of mover, because the distance over which a person travels can also be used as a proxy for other important variables'. As cost is a significant factor in the distance over which migration takes place, the relative distance of movements may have a filtering effect upon the kinds of people who are moving between different areas. There is also a broad relationship between social/cultural change and distance. A change of dialect or differences in the social organisation of groups may make the migrant seem an obvious 'outsider'. To avoid such changes the prospective migrant may decide on a shorter distance movement. Long distance movement may also involve entry into areas with different ethnicity, colour or religion, all of which may hinder the process of assimilation.

In terms of direction, the most prevalent forms of migration are from rural to urban environments and from peripheral regions to core regions. Thus the main migration streams are from culturally traditional areas to areas where rapid change is taking place. In LEDCs the socio-economic differences between rural and urban areas are generally of a much greater magnitude than in MEDCs.

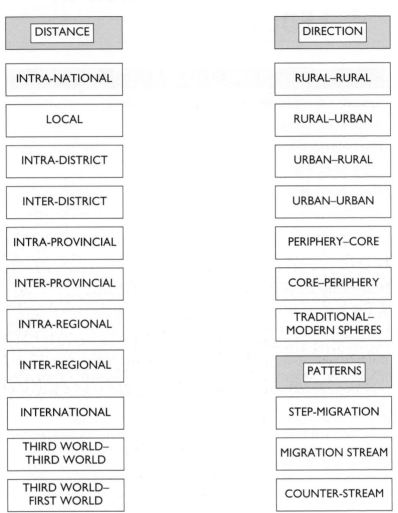

Figure 11 Spatial dimensions of population movement in LEDCs
Source: Population Movements and the Third World by M. Parnwell,
Routledge, 1993

Although of a lesser magnitude, rural to rural migration is common in LEDCs for a variety of reasons including employment, family reunion or marriage. In some instances governments have encouraged the agricultural development of frontier areas such as the Amazon basin (Figure 12).

Movements between urban areas consist of step-migration up the urban hierarchy as migrants improve their knowledge base and financial position, adding to a range of other urban–urban migrations for reasons such as employment and education. Urban–rural

Figure 12 Rural to rural migration: farmers who migrated from North East Brazil harvesting crops in the Amazon basin

migration is dominated by counterstream movement, i.e. urbanites who are returning to their rural origins.

b) The temporal perspective

Figure 13 provides a useful classification of population movement in LEDCs in terms of the time spent away from home. Clearly, all movements involving a change of residence for a year or more should be termed migration. However, some of the movements in Figure 13,

Time-span	Type of movement	Characteristics
SHORT-TERM		
A few hours	Oscillation	Farmwork; collecting (fuelwood, water)
Daily	Commuting	Journey to work, education, market
Weekly	Commuting	Away during the working week; entertainment, worship
Season	Seasonal circulation	Nomadism, pastoralism, transhumance; seasonal employment
Periodic	Sojourn	Hunting and gathering; trading, visiting
Once in a lifetime	Pilgrimage	Pilgrimage, marriage; displacement by natural disaster
Yearly	Contract labour migration	Target migration
Several years	Shifting cultivation	Shifting cultivation, frontier settlement
Working life	Temporary circulation	Urban-bound employment-related migration
Lifetime	Permanent migration	Emigration, resettlement, refugee movements
LONG-TERM		

Figure 13 Temporal dimensions of population movements in LEDCs
Source: Population Movements and the Third World, M. Parnwell, Routledge, 1993

which are usually less than a year in duration, may under certain circumstances last longer than this. The most obvious examples here are nomadism and pilgrimage.

c) The motivational perspective

Petersen's typology, presented in Chapter 2, provides a useful framework for discussion on why people migrate. The most important distinction is between voluntary and involuntary migration. In terms of the former it is useful to differentiate between *independent* and *dependent* movements. In independent movements the decision to move to a new location is made by the individual, whereas in dependent movements the decision is taken collectively by the household. In the latter case the individual concerned may or may not have a significant say in the final decision, often depending on the age of the prospective migrant.

In LEDCs forced recruitment of labour suggests that the incidence of free migration has been limited. Even in recent times the scale of involuntary movement in LEDCs is considerably higher than most people think. However, giving due consideration to such movements should not blind us to the increasing scale of free labour migration that has occurred in recent decades.

In the latter part of the twentieth century some of the world's most violent and protracted conflicts have been in LEDCs, particularly in Africa (e.g. Angola, Mozambique and Rwanda) and Asia (e.g. Vietnam, Cambodia and Afghanistan). These troubles have led to numerous population movements of a significant scale. Not all have crossed international frontiers to merit the term 'refugee' movements. Instead, many have involved internal displacement. This is a major global problem which is showing little sign of abatement.

Many LEDCs are prone to natural disasters. Because poor nations do not possess the funds to minimise the consequences of natural disaster as MEDCs can, forced migration is often the result. Some LEDCs have been devastated time and time again, often eliciting only a minimal response from the outside world. Examples include drought in Ethiopia and flooding in Bangladesh.

Increasingly large numbers of people have been displaced by major infrastructural projects and by the commercial sector's huge appetite for land. In LEDCs the protests of communities in the way of 'progress' are invariably ignored for reasons of 'national interest' or pure greed. The World Bank and other international organisations have been heavily criticised in recent decades for financing numerous large scale projects without giving sufficient consideration to those people directly affected.

2 The causes of migration

The reasons why people change their place of permanent residence can be viewed at three dimensions of scale: macro-level, meso-level and micro-level.

a) The macro-level

This dimension highlights socio-economic differences at the national scale, focusing particularly on the core-periphery concept. The development of core regions in many LEDCs has its origins in the colonial era which was characterised by the selective and incomplete opening-up of territories, supporting development in a restricted range of economic sectors. At this time migration was encouraged to supply labour for new colonial enterprises and infrastructural projects such as the development of ports and the construction of transport links between areas of raw material exploitation and the ports through which export would take place.

The introduction of capitalism, through colonialism, into previously non-capitalist societies had a huge influence on population movement patterns. The demand for labour in mines, plantations and other activities was satisfied to a considerable extent by coercing people into migration to work either directly through forced labour systems or indirectly through taxation. The spread of a cash economy into peripheral areas further increased the need for paid employment which, on the whole, could only be found in the economic core region.

In the post-colonial era most LEDCs have looked to industrialisation as their path to a better world, resulting in disproportionate investment in the urban industrial sector and the relative neglect of the rural economy. Even where investment in agriculture has been considerable, either the objective or the end result was to replace labour with machinery, adding further to rural out-migration.

This macro-level perspective, provides a general explanation of migration patterns in LEDCs. However, this approach has two weaknesses:

1. It fails to explain why some people migrate and others stay put when faced with very similar circumstances in peripheral areas.
2. It offers no explanation as to why all forms of migration do not occur in the direction of economic core regions.

b) The meso-level

The meso-level dimension includes more detailed consideration of the factors at the origin and destination which influence people's migration decisions. Lee's origin-intervening obstacles-destination model, which was discussed in Chapter 2, is a useful starting point in understanding this level of approach, which looks well beyond economic factors and recognises the vital role of the perception of the individual in the decision-making process.

Lee argues that migration occurs in response to the prevailing set of factors both in the migrant's place of origin and in one or a number of potential destinations. However, what is perceived as positive and what is viewed as negative at the origin and destination may vary considerably between individuals, as may the intervening obstacles. As Lee states 'It is not so much the actual factors at origin and destination as the perception of these factors which result in migration. Personal sensitivities, intelligence and awareness of conditions elsewhere enter into the evaluation of the situation at origin, and knowledge of the situation at destination depends upon personal contacts or upon sources of information which are not universally available. In addition, there are personalities which are resistant to change and there are personalities which welcome change for the sake of change. For some individuals, there must be compelling reasons for migration, while for others little provocation or promise suffices'. Lee stressed the point that the factors in favour of migration would generally have to outweigh considerably those against due to the natural reluctance of people to uproot themselves from established communities.

While recognising that individuals can react differently to similar circumstances it is still important to consider the negative factors which act to 'push' people from rural areas of origin and the positive influences which 'pull' them towards towns and cities. In Brazil the push factors responsible for rural to urban migration can be summarised as follows:

- The mechanisation of agriculture which has reduced the demand for farm labour in most parts of the country.
- The amalgamation of farms and estates, particularly by agricultural production companies. In Brazil, as elsewhere in South America, the high incidence of landlessness has led to a much greater level of rural to urban migration compared to most parts of Africa and Asia.
- The generally poor conditions of rural employment. Employers often ignore laws relating to minimum wages and other employee rights.
- Desertification in the North East and deforestation in the North.
- Unemployment and underemployment.
- Poor social conditions particularly in terms of housing, health and education.

High population growth is often cited as the major cause of rural to urban migration. However, in itself population growth is not the main cause of out-migration. Its effects have to be seen in conjunction with the failure of other processes to provide adequately for the needs of growing rural communities. Even when governments focus resources on rural development the volume of out-migration may not be reduced. The irony in many LEDCs is that people are being displaced from the countryside because in some areas change is too slow to accommodate the growing size and needs of the population, or because in other areas change is too quick to enable redundant rural workers to find alternative employment in their home areas. In such circumstances out-migration does indeed provide an essential 'safety-valve'. However, as Parnwell asserts 'We should be careful not to see migration as the only choice open to rural folk who find themselves faced with such difficulties. People may respond by adapting to their changing circumstances, or they may organise themselves politically and economically in order to confront whatever forces are responsible for their plight.'

The evidence in Figure 14 and in other similar studies is that economic motives underpin the majority of rural to urban movements. During the 1960s most demographers cited higher wages and more varied employment opportunities in the cities as the prime reason for internal migration. It was also widely held that the level of migration was strongly related to the rate of urban unemployment. However, while rural/urban income differentials are easy to quantify, they do not take into account the lower cost of living in the countryside and the fact that non-cash income often forms a significant proportion of rural incomes.

In the 1970s, as more and more cities in LEDCs experienced large

(a) Reasons for migration from village communities in rural Peru

Reason	Percentage of respondents citing reason
To earn more money	39
To join kin already working	25
No work in the villages	12
Work opportunities presented themselves	11
Dislike of village life	11
To be near the village and family	11
To support nuclear and/or extended family	9
Poor	8
To pay for education	7

Source: Julian Laite (1988) 'The migrant response in central Peru', in Josef Gugler (ed.), The Urbanization of the Third World. Oxford: Oxford University Press.

(b) Principal reasons for migration from village communities in north-east Thailand

Principal reason	Number of respondents citing reason	Percentage of respondents citing reason
To earn more money for the household	138	52.9
To earn more money for self	57	21.8
To earn more money for parents	31	11.9
To further education	12	4.6
To earn money to build a house	10	3.8
To earn money to invest in farming	4	1.5
For fun	3	1.1
To earn money to purchase land/land title	2	0.8
To earn money to repay a debt	1	0.4
To earn money to pay for hired labour	1	0.4
To see Bangkok	1	0.4
To earn money to get married	1	0.4
Total:	261	100.0

Figure 14 Reasons for migration from rural areas in (a) Peru and (b) Thailand
Source: Population Movements and the Third World, M. Parnwell, Routledge, 1993

scale in-migration in spite of high unemployment, demographers began to reappraise the situation. Todaro was one of the first to recognise that the paradox of urban deprivation on the one hand and migration in pursuit of higher wages on the other could be explained by taking a long term view of why people move to urban areas. As the more detailed consideration of the Todaro Model in Chapter 2 explains, people are prepared to ensure urban hardship in the short term in the likelihood that their long term prospects will be much better in the city compared to the countryside. Apart from employment prospects the other perceived advantages of the cities include a higher standard of accommodation, a better education for migrants' children, improved medical facilities, infrastructure often lacking in rural areas and a wider range of consumer services. The most fortunate migrants find jobs in the formal sector. A regular wage then gives some access to the other advantages of urban life. However, as the demand for jobs greatly outstrips supply, many can do no better than the uncertainty of the informal sector.

Of all the factors that migrants take into account before arriving at a decision, the economic perspective invariably dominates the decision to leave the countryside. However, all the evidence shows that other factors, particularly the social environment, have a very strong influence on the direction that the movement takes. This largely explains why capital cities, with their wide range of social opportunities, attract so many rural migrants.

c) The micro-level

The main criticisms of the macro and meso-scale explanations of migration are that:

1. They view migration as a passive response to a variety of stimuli.
2. They tend to view rural source areas as an undifferentiated entity.

The specific circumstances of individual families and communities in terms of urban contact are of crucial importance in the decision to move, particularly when long distances are involved. The alienation experienced by the new migrant to an urban area should not be underestimated and is something that will be avoided if at all possible. The evidence comes from a significant number of sample surveys and from the high incidence of 'area of origin' communities found in cities. For example:

- A sample survey of rural migrants in Bombay found that more than 75% already had one or more relatives living in the city, from whom 90% had received some form of assistance upon arrival.
- A survey of migration from the Peruvian Highlands to Lima found that 90% of migrants could rely on short term accommodation on arrival in the city, and for about half, their contacts had managed to arrange a job for them.

The importance of established links between urban and rural areas frequently results in the phenomenon of 'chain migration'. After one or a small number of pioneering migrants have led the way subsequent waves of migration from the same rural community follow. The more established a migrant community becomes in the city the easier it appears to be for others in the rural community to take the decision to move and for them to assimilate into urban society.

Apart from contact with, and knowledge of urban locations, differentiation between rural households takes the following forms:

- level of income
- size of land holding
- size of household
- stage in the life cycle
- level of education
- cohesiveness of the family unit.

All of these factors impact on the decision to migrate. Family ties and commitments may determine whether or not someone is able to migrate, and may also influence who from a family unit is most likely to take on the responsibility of seeking employment in the city. Here the stage in the life cycle is crucial and it is not surprising that the great majority of migrants in LEDCs are aged between 15 and 25 years. In some communities the phenomenon of 'relay migration' has been identified whereby at different stages in a family's life cycle, different people take responsibility for migration.

It is only by examining all three dimensions, macro, meso and micro, that the complexity of the migration process can be fully understood. As elsewhere in geographical analysis there is a tendency to over-simplify. This is often useful in the early stages of enquiry but such generalisations may mask essential detail.

3 The characteristics of migrants

Migration is a selective process which is influenced by economic, social, cultural, political and environmental factors. All of these influences are subject to change over time, partly under the influence of migration itself. Global generalisations about migration in LEDCs can be made but in virtually every case exceptions can be found. The main generalisations that can be made about the characteristics of migrants based on a range of studies in different countries are:

- Most surveys show that rural migrants are predominantly young adult males, although the degree of gender bias has decreased over time.
- Due to the segmentation of migration streams, migrants tend to come from specific areas. Once segmentation is in place it tends to reinforce itself as migration networks 'mature'.
- Migrants are not necessarily the poorest people from rural areas, particularly not when the migratory jobs are attractive and have significantly higher returns than staying in the rural community.
- The poorest areas do not usually have the highest rates of out-migration, as has been shown for China by Mallee (1996) and for Indian villages by Connell et al (1976).

- A large proportion of migrants maintain regular contact with their area of origin resulting in counterstreams at varying levels of intensity.

a) Gender differences in rural to urban migration

In recent decades gender has come to occupy a significant place in the migration literature. This has made a crucial contribution to our understanding of migration processes. According to de Haan 'There is now much more emphasis on the differential migration responses by men and women, which themselves are context dependent, and on gender discrimination in returns to migrant labour'.

Recent research has extended the Todaro Model by suggesting that males receive larger monetary returns than females as a result of migration and consequently have a greater incentive to move to urban areas. In a study of rural to urban migration in Kenya, Agesa and Agesa found that rural men are significantly more educated than rural women and hence will migrate to urban areas in greater numbers as urban jobs generally demand higher educational requirements than those in rural areas. In addition the urban–rural wage gap is larger for males than females giving higher economic returns for migration to men. Taking these two factors together it is perhaps not surprising that women constitute only 21% of public and private sector wage employment in the urban areas of Kenya (1991).

The foundations of gender differences in migration in Kenya were laid before independence in 1963. Before independence women were barred from migrating to urban areas and these restrictions helped to create a pattern of migration that is pervasive in Kenya today. The high rate of fertility in Kenya, one of the highest in the world, also reduces the likelihood of female migration. Child-rearing over a long period of time and the responsibility of looking after a large family inevitably reduce the propensity to migrate. On the other hand, for many families it makes male migration all the more necessary. Although women account for 56% of the country's population, approximately 87% live in rural areas compared to 54% of men.

In contrast, in South America, recent studies show that women equal or outnumber men in urban migration streams and that the majority of women are economically active in their urban destinations. However, a higher percentage of women than men work in the informal sector where incomes are low and labour protection poor. An important stimulus to female rural to urban migration has been an increase in the type of industrial jobs which employers see as being particularly suitable for women. The establishment of free trade zones and export-led growth strategies have added to this effect. Radcliffe's study of peasant households in the Peruvian province of Calca in the southern Andes found that one-third of eldest daughters had out-migrated compared to only 14% of sons. This is largely because in this region women are considered as marginal to agricultural work and therefore as 'surplus' labour. Similarly, research by Gilbert et al. (1994) in the Campoo and Misque provinces of Bolivia shows that young unmarried women in rural peasant households are frequently migratory. Two influences are dominant here: the importance for women to bring a dowry to their marriage and inheritance patterns which have favoured passing scarce land to male offspring.

Singh (1984) found higher rates of female rural to urban migration in southern India compared to northern India. Singh relates this to Boserup's 1970 study of women's role in economic development, noting that the pattern of female participation in northern India resembles that of women in West Asian and North African Arab countries, whereas the pattern in southern India is similar to that of South East Asia. Her analysis emphasises cultural reasons, in particular northern Indian practices related to seclusion of women that affect female migration and employment.

b) Family and community influences on migration

Findlay (1997) stresses the complexity of family-migration interactions and describes how six essential features of the African family structure condition migration patterns and vice versa:

- The extended family structure facilitates migration.
- Male–female segregation of roles makes it unremarkable for men and women to migrate and set up separate residences.
- The dominance of lineage over conjugal relations help migration decisions to be made in a wider household or clan context.
- Polygamy increases the need to earn cash for bride price and maintain a larger family.
- Dominance by elders sometimes makes young adults migrate to escape their control.

Ethnographic analysis has played a very important role in the growing understanding of gender differences in migration and the influence of the household in decision-making. According to McHugh (2000) 'the characteristic feature of ethnographic research is the illumination of human experience and the human condition within a socio-cultural frame.'

The characteristics of migrants are crucial to the impact of migration on economic and social development in areas of origin and destination. Our understanding of this important aspect of migration has improved considerably as research has moved beyond individual motivation to consider the significant influences of family and community.

4 The effects of migration

(a) Migrant incomes and remittances

Figure 15 provides a useful framework for understanding the costs and returns from migration. It highlights the main factors which determine how rural areas are affected by migration – namely the two-

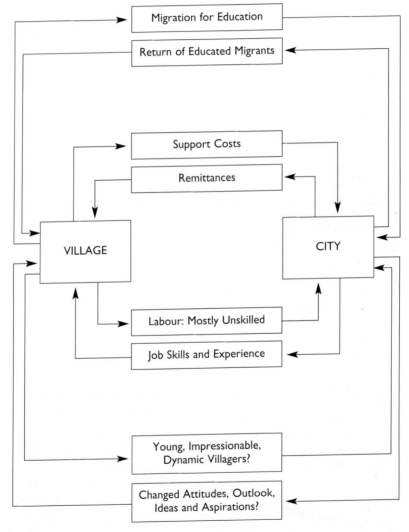

Figure 15 The costs and returns from migration
Source: Population Movements and the Third World, M. Parnwell, Routledge, 1993

way transfers of labour, money, skills and attitudes. However, while all of the linkages seem obvious, none are easy to quantify. Therefore, apart from very clear-cut cases, it is often difficult to decide which is greater – the costs or benefits of migration.

Remittances from internal migration are even more difficult to estimate than those arising from international migration. Thus, it is not surprising that research has produced a wide range of conclusions of which the following are but a sample:

- Williamson (1988) put urban-rural remittances at 10–13% of urban incomes in Africa.
- Reardon (1997) noted that in rural areas not close to major cities in Africa migrant earnings accounted for only 20% of total non-farm earnings, whereas it reached as high as 75% of total non-farm earnings in areas close to major cities.
- Rempell and Lobdell (1978) concluded that remittances constituted up to 40% of the income of rural households.
- Adepoju and Mbugua (1997) note that migrants often remit up to 60% of their incomes.

However, it is important to note that the flow of money and support in general is not always one-way. Some studies have highlighted village-to-town remittances to support education or the search for employment.

De la Briere et al. (1997) note two types of economic model that attempt to explain remittance behaviour. The first model focuses on the notion of an insurance contract between the migrant and the household left behind, as a means of coping with household risk. A variation on this approach sees migration and remittances as a form of 'portfolio diversification' where potential remittances are weighed against the returns from local sources of income. The second model is based on the bequest motive, seeing remittances as investments in household assets that the migrant will later inherit.

Helweg (1983) studied the changing use of remittances over time, noting three stages: initially they are spent on family maintenance and improving land productivity; in the following stage spending tends to be on 'conspicuous' consumption (for example fridge, furniture, television); in the third and final stage remittances are also invested to start commercial, non-agricultural activities. Vijverberg and Zeager (1994) found that in Tanzania migrant workers in both public and private sectors initially received lower wages than native urban workers but the wage gap was eliminated in a decade or less.

b) Migration and development

The relationship between migration and development is complex and still the subject of much debate. The four questions which have been the subject of much research are:

1. How does development in areas of destination affect migration?
2. How does development in the area of origin affect migration?
3. How does migration affect development in areas of destination?
4. How does migration affect development in the area of origin?

The first question is the least problematic. The importance of pull factors in explaining both national and international movements is widely accepted. Clearly migrants do move in reaction to newly developed opportunities. However, a number of recent studies have shown that people in the poorest areas of LEDCs do not exhibit the highest levels of out-migration. In such regions, levels of literacy and skill may be so low that access to even very menial urban jobs may be difficult.

It is in many ways ironic that development in rural areas of origin often acts as a stimulus to out-migration. In China the development of rural enterprises appears to increase rates of out-migration. In the Punjab, the Green Revolution witnessed both high rates of out-migration by the resident population and in-migration from a number of poorer Indian states. Development often acts as an important stimulus, widening the horizons of the rural population.

There is some evidence that internal migration in LEDCs is welfare-improving for receiving regions but quantification has generally proved to be difficult. The fact that rural migrants are often the most dynamic young adults from their communities should be of benefit to the receiving urban areas, provided enough opportunities are available for most to gain reasonable employment. On the one hand the influx of rural labour provides the foundation for industrialisation and other forms of economic development. On the other, newcomers can place a massive burden on over-stretched urban amenities and services, particularly if large numbers are unemployed.

The impact of out-migration on areas of origin is not at all clear. The traditional view has been that by reducing unemployment and underemployment, and providing inputs such as remittances and newly acquired skills, migration promotes development in rural areas of origin, narrows regional disparities and eventually makes migration unnecessary. However, recent research on this issue has in some respects been contradictory, and the possibility of such mobility having an adverse effect on the economy of labour-exporting areas cannot be ruled out. Mukherji (1985) argues that circulation of Indian wage labourers 'occurs within, and in turn reinforces, the syndrome of poverty and mobility'. Lipton, with reference to the Indian Village Studies Programme, emphasised the inequality-increasing effects of rural to urban migration in areas of origin. High emigration from a village is strongly related to the unequal distribution of resources, usually land. Migration frequently involves both the richest and poorest households in the village. Richer potential migrants are 'pulled' towards firm job prospects in the formal sector whereas the poor are 'pushed' by rural poverty and labour-replacing methods. The much higher remittances from rich migrants compared to poorer migrants from the same community increases inequalities in villages and between villages in the same region. The main conclusion that can be drawn from this, and other recent research is that although migration in many cases does alleviate poverty, it can also increase inequality.

An important issue is the impact of out-migration on local agriculture. The key questions here are

1. What effect does the loss of a significant number of young adult males have on agricultural production?
2. If the impact is negative can it be offset by the positive effects of remittances and ideas brought back by returning migrants?

In some cases out-migration undoubtedly causes a shortage of labour, although in other instances it clearly alleviates unemployment and underemployment. In some areas large numbers of women now perform agricultural tasks which were once the preserve of men. This 'new' work is frequently in addition to an existing heavy household workload. Although remittances help they are often too low to hire labour. There is also a tendency for land to become concentrated in the hands of migrant families who gradually turn into non-farmers resulting in a fall in agricultural production.

It seems that for every study that highlights the negative impact of out-migration on local agriculture, a research project can be found that emphasises the positive impact. The use of remittances to purchase new machinery and the diffusion of new farming and business techniques into rural areas as migrants return has transformed agriculture in some areas. Whether the impact of out-migration on agriculture is positive or negative depends on the complex interaction of a range of social and economic factors which may be subject to change over time.

5 Policies and planning

A UN survey conducted in 1978 established that 116 out of the 122 LEDCs studied had devised policies to reduce the rate of rural to urban migration. Clearly the individual benefits derived from migration have, cumulatively over time, resulted in significant social costs.

Figure 16 summarises the main policy responses to migration which, over the past 40 years have moved away from the draconian to the more realistic and humane.

a) Negative approaches

Largely a thing of the past, such approaches were mainly used by authoritarian governments concerned with the perceived negative effects of large scale rural to urban migration. However, governments

Policy approaches	Rationale	Types of policies and programmes
Negative	Emphasizes the undesirability of migration and seeks to erect barriers to population movement and to forcibly 'deport' migrants	Closed city; pass laws; deportation of beggars, the homeless and those in marginal occupations; bull-dozing of squatter settlements; enforced resettlement from urban to rural areas; sedentarization of nomads; registration systems; employment controls; restricted access to housing; food rationing systems; benign neglect.
Accommodative	Accepts migration as inevitable, and seeks to minimize the negative effects in both origin and destination places	Slum up-grading; sites and services; urban job creation – labour-intensive industrialization; minimum wage legislation; urban skills training; urban infra-structural investment; improved social welfare; improvements in transportation; relieving congestion.
Manipulative	Accepts migration as inevitable and even desirable in some cases but seeks to redirect migration flows towards alternative destinations	Colonization; land settlement; land development; polarization reversal; growth poles; urban, industrial and administrative decentralization; information systems; management of contact networks.
Preventive	Rather than dealing with the symptoms of migration, attempts to confront the root causes by tackling poverty, inequality and unemployment at source, and reducing the attractiveness of urban areas to potential migrants	Land reform; agricultural intensification; agricultural extension; rural infrastructural investment; rural industrialization; rural minimum wages legislation; rural job creation; improving rural–urban terms of trade; reducing urban bias; increased emphasis in 'bottom-up' planning; propaganda in favour of the rural sector.

Figure 16 Migration policy approaches
Source: Population Movements and the Third World, M. Parnwell,
Routledge, 1993

in some LEDCs continue to make life very difficult for migrants in the hope that they will eventually return to their rural areas. Perhaps the best example is the use of migration controls in the People's Republic of China which will be discussed in the case study section at the end of this chapter.

There are other significant examples worthy of mention at this stage. During the Vietnam War, the government in Saigon attempted to reduce the large scale movement of rural peasants into the city through a policy of benign neglect. The theory was that the more intolerable conditions became in the city, the fewer people would be inclined to make the journey. However, this policy was largely destined to failure due to the severe disruption that was occurring in the countryside because of the war.

In 1970, Jakarta, the capital of Indonesia was declared a 'closed city'. To gain access to the city prospective migrants had to get permission to leave their home area and obtain a 'short visit' card. Additionally they were required to deposit with the authorities twice the fare to Jakarta (which was a very large sum of money indeed for most rural dwellers). Deposits were returned if, within six months, migrants could provide proof of accommodation and employment. They would then be given an identity card confirming them as citizens of Jakarta. Those who could not fulfil these requirements were 'deported' from the city.

In Ethiopia, from the overthrow of Haille Selassie and the Socialist Revolution in 1974, up until the 1990s, a major strand of government policy was to control population movement. During this period 'voluntary' migration was much lower in Ethiopia than in the rest of sub-Saharan Africa, and it was not until the lifting of restrictions in the late 1990s that migration was made easier. At the same time 'involuntary' politically-induced population displacement and resettlement occurred on an unprecedented scale and led to enormous population shifts, largely within rural areas.

Since 1964, the Castro regime in Cuba has practised a 'return to the land' movement which has resulted in the population of Havana remaining virtually the same in the intervening period. The two-pronged approach was to restrict freedom of movement to the capital city and to promote the 'urbanisation of the countryside' thereby reducing the desire of rural dwellers to move.

The use of such negative approaches to rural to urban migration has declined over the years for three reasons: they are difficult to implement, they are extremely unpopular among the people they seek to contain, and they are seen as inhumane and anti-democratic in the outside world.

b) Accommodative approaches

The accommodative approach seeks to minimise the negative affects of movement in both rural and urban areas. It recognises the positive attributes of movement such as its role in redistributing income from urban to rural areas, its potential contribution to industrialisation and its importance to the development of urban-rural linkages.

In rural areas the emphasis is often on education and training. While this might encourage a degree of movement, those that leave the rural environment are more likely to gain reasonable employment in the city. In urban areas policies focus on improving the welfare of newcomers to the city through such measures as minimum wage legislation, regulations concerning working conditions, and job creation programmes. For example, in Malaysia the authorities in urban areas help street sellers by providing training, capital and marketing assistance. In other countries such as Peru and South Africa, squatter settlements have been legalised and the threat of eviction removed.

The positive side of this approach lies in its humanity. However it has been criticised for two reasons:

1. Like the negative approach it deals with the symptoms of migration rather than its causes.
2. It does not dissuade, and may in fact encourage greater movement towards urban areas, actually adding to the existing problem.

c) Manipulative approaches

The fundamental objective of this type of approach is to direct economic growth to smaller intermediate cities and towns further down the urban hierarchy. The result should be a reduction in pressure on the capital city and a more even spread of employment around the country. Hence most potential migrants should be within relatively easy reach of a regional growth pole. An increased volume of short distance local movement will not only support the development of activities in smaller provincial and regional centres but also strengthen the linkages between these urban settlements and their rural hinterlands. An important part of this strategy, which reached the height of its popularity during the 1970s and early 1980s, is to ensure that potential migrants are aware of the new opportunities in regional growth poles. Some countries, notably Brazil and Pakistan, went as far as establishing new capital cities in order to reduce the pressure of population movement on one core region and to achieve a more even spread of economic growth.

In Venezuela the government used revenue from petroleum exports to construct the new town of Ciudad Guyana in the poor south-eastern part of the country to act as a counterweight to the capital Caracas. The new town became so popular that housing was soon in short supply, leading to the development of squatter settlements. Amid rising concern about the phenomenal growth of Bangkok, the government of Thailand embarked on an ambitious regional policy aimed at directing investment away from the capital. Investors were offered a package of financial incentives, including an 8-year tax exemption in regions outside Bangkok. In addition, two development zones, 80 km and 120 km south-east of Bangkok, were established in 1981. The prime objective was to attract $4 billion of investment and draw off industry from Bangkok.

In most countries the outcome of decentralisation policies proved to be disappointing, resulting in substantial policy modifications during the 1980s and 1990s. The new strategy adopted by a number of countries has been to promote shorter-distance movements to satellite towns around the main urban centres. Mexico and South Korea provide successful examples of such policies. However, the obvious criticism of the new strategy was that although it helped to contain growth in the capital city itself, it did nothing to deflect growth from the economic core region in general.

d) Preventive approaches

The philosophy of this type of approach is to confront the main reasons for migration from rural areas – land, employment and income. A number of LEDCs have introduced programmes of land reform. The objective here is to redistribute land, giving the landless the potential to earn a reasonable living from farming.

In Brazil, the distribution of land in terms of ownership has been a divisive issue since the colonial era. During this time the monarchy rewarded those in favour with huge tracts of land, leaving a legacy of highly concentrated ownership. Today 44% of all arable land in Brazil is owned by just 1% of the nation's farmers, while 15 million peasants own little or no land. Many of these peasants are impoverished, roving migrants who have lost their jobs as agricultural labourers due to the spread of mechanisation. Although successive governments have vowed to tackle the land problem, progress has been limited due to the economic and political power of the 'fazenda' or farm-owners. The latter have not been slow to use aggressive tactics, legal or otherwise, to evict squatters and delay expropriation. Their actions have included bribing and intimidating members of the judiciary and land-reform officials in order to keep their large estates intact.

In the mid-1990s land reform clearly emerged as Brazil's leading social problem, highlighted by a number of widely publicised squatter invasions. The most organised occupations were led by sophisticated groups of peasants and sympathisers (left-wing politicians, trade unionists and Catholic clergy), known as the MST, Movimento Sem Terra. While most occupations were peaceful, more than 200 peasants were killed by police in land conflicts around the country. The election of the left-wing intellectual, Henrique Cardoso in 1994, gave added impetus to the land reform movement. In 1995, 42,000 families were settled on land which was new to them with government aid. In 1996 Congress approved a rural land tax aimed at landowners of unproductive properties. Land considered unproductive, and whose owners did not pay the new tax, was confiscated by the state after five years and included in the agrarian reform programme. Liquidated banks also became a new source of land for agrarian reform. In 1996 The National Land Reform Agency purchased over 24,000 hectares of land with the assets of the failed Banorte and Banco Economico. This was to provide small farms for 1000 landless families.

However, policies which at first seem successful may not stem out-migration in the long term. The break-up of sugar plantations in the coastal regions of Peru in the late 1960s and early 1970s and the establishment of agricultural cooperatives witnessed a considerable rise in productivity. However, as efficiency increased, the demand for labour declined with most of the jobless turning to the cities in their search for new employment.

Some development strategists see rural industrialisation as the main tool for limiting rural–urban migration. A number of Asian countries in particular have adopted this approach with mixed results. In Thailand the government has given high priority to its 'industrialisation of the countryside' policy. This includes the modernisation of cottage industries and the establishment of 'putting-out' systems where rural households become involved in parts of the manufacturing process for urban-based industries. This programme has achieved a reasonable level of success and contrasts with Indian attempts to upgrade cottage industry which in some areas led to an increase in out-migration as rural skill levels improved.

In Sri Lanka the emphasis has been on reducing the welfare gap between the rural and urban areas by improving rural medical and educational facilities, by providing income support for farmers in the form of guaranteed prices, and by upgrading low income rural housing. Because of the importance of perception in the decision to migrate the government has advertised its policies heavily in rural areas with a reasonable degree of success.

Case study: Internal migration in China

Recent economic change in China has unleashed a huge rural to urban migration on a scale probably never before experienced anywhere in the world. The full consequences of such a vast movement will become more apparent in the coming years. For some time China has had a fear of uncontrolled population movement. Since the Chinese Communist Party came to power in 1949, regulating and controlling migration has been one of China's most consistent development policies. From the 1950s the main instrument used to control rural to urban migration has been the population register system which identified people as either 'urban' or 'rural'. Permission was required to leave the countryside and was only given if potential migrants could produce documentary evidence that they had an urban job to go to. Food rationing was also used to restrict movement from the countryside. Grain and oil rations in the cities were made available only to people in possession of urban household registration documents.

Alongside these measures, since the 1950s the authorities have periodically encouraged large numbers of people to leave the cities. Some have done so voluntarily, others very reluctantly. In the 1950s and 1960s significant numbers of people were sent from urban areas to develop oil-fields in northern and north-eastern China, and to colonise new land for cereal cultivation. The government was also keen to increase population in the sparsely peopled western provinces in an effort to achieve more balanced regional development and for reasons of national security. In total the main migratory direction in China at this time was from the densely populated central and eastern provinces to the sparsely populated and remote border provincial regions in the northern and western parts of the country. Heilongjiang, Inner Mongolia, Xinjiang, Quinghai and Ningxia in particular received large numbers of migrants.

The 'back to the villages' movement in the early 1960s saw 20 million people leave large cities to return to their rural origins. Alongside this counterstream, large scale deportations of urban youth to the countryside occurred from the mid-1950s onwards. Between 1969 and 1973 alone an estimated 10 to 15 million urban school leavers were resettled in rural areas. The twin objectives were to relieve urban pressure and to improve rural productivity. The latter would be achieved by the higher level of education the young urbanites would bring to the countryside. Thus, in contrast to the situation in many LEDCs, in-migration accounted for only about 30% of urban growth in China during the 1950s, 1960s and 1970s.

This unpopular process continued until the late 1970s after which it was reversed in support of China's industrialisation strategy. The emphasis on regional development shifted to the coastal regions to speed up economic development there. As a result many coastal regions such as Jiangsu, Zhejiang and Guangdang experienced rapid population and economic growth. The relaxation of controls on rural to urban migration in the 1980s resulted in rapid urbanisation. The huge increase in construction projects attracted many rural migrants but there was huge competition for every job in the formal sector leaving many disappointed and forced to scratch a living in the informal sector.

A large number of towns and cities have emerged, while old cities have rapidly expanded their administrative areas. The number of towns increased from 2819 in 1982 to 17,282 by 1995, while the number of cities rose from 191 in 1978 to 640 by 1995. Shanghai increased its urban area from 141 Km^2 to just over

Year	Urban (m)	Rural (m)	China (m)	Urban (%)
1988	334.40	766.44	1100.84	30.38
1990	367.40	768.51	1135.91	32.34
1995	450.04	778.57	1228.61	36.63
2000	530.51	781.49	1312.00	40.44
2010	702.50	725.12	1427.61	49.21
2020	875.66	654.56	1530.22	57.22
2030	1015.66	578.95	1594.61	63.69
2040	1122.59	481.01	1603.60	70.00
2060	1233.56	306.86	1540.42	80.08
2087	1218.53	151.02	1369.55	88.97

Figure 17 Urban and rural population in China
Source: China's Future Population and Development Challenges –
J. Shen, The Geographical Journal Vol 164, No 1, March 1998

230 Km² by establishing two new urban districts, Wusong in 1980 and Minhang in 1982, and to 350 Km² by the expansion of existing districts. The establishment of Pudong in 1990 added some 350 Km² to the urban area of Shanghai, providing more development space for China's leading economic centre. Overall, the urban population in China is expected to rise from 450 million in 1995 to 1123 million by 2040 (Figure 17).

A major consequence of such rapid urban growth is the loss of arable land, as so many of the largest urban areas are located in rich agricultural districts. At present 0.3–0.4 million hectares of arable land a year are being lost to urban land uses. However, it has been estimated that grain production must be increased by at least 4.47 million Kg per year over the next 25 years to keep up with the growing population. There is an urgent need to review the process of land management and to control the transfer of agricultural land to other uses.

Although considerable changes in migration restrictions were introduced in the early 1980s, the household registration system was not dismantled and it continues to provide the framework within which migration takes place. Local authorities in rural areas continue their efforts to limit out-migration while local governments in city destinations have erected barriers in terms of employment discrimination and the 'deportation' of migrants back to their areas of origin. Without urban household registration, migrants cannot get access to schooling, health care and housing. This is why migrants rarely bring their families with them when they seek work in the cities. Many migrants are kept in 'welfare' centres akin to detention camps. These are at the heart of the authorities 'custody and repatriation' policies which sanction arbitrary detention that bypasses the judicial process. Human Rights in China, an organisation based in New York estimates that

	Employment	Study and training	Joining family	Retirement	Marriage	Other causes
Intra-provincial in-migration						
City	33.7	15.3	27.7	1.1	13.8	8.5
Town	31.5	6.6	26.3	1.8	25.4	8.4
County	9.9	0.3	13.9	4.3	65.2	6.3
Subtotal	27.2	8.0	23.9	2.2	30.8	7.9
Inter-provincial in-migration						
City	41.6	16.4	32.2	1.8	4.8	3.2
Town	36.8	1.3	36.6	2.5	16.0	6.7
County	18.7	0.5	27.7	4.1	37.1	11.8
Subtotal	34.7	9.0	32.0	2.5	15.5	6.2
Total	28.8	8.2	25.6	2.3	27.7	7.6

Note: Migrations (transitions) refer to the period 1982–1987.

Figure 18 Proportion of migrants by various causes (%)
Source: Internal Migration and Regional Population Dynamics in China – Jianfa Shen, Progess in Planning, Vol 45, Part 3, 1996

several million rural migrants a year are locked up for varying time periods under this procedure. A recent Survey of China in the Economist (April 2000) concluded that 'the discrimination against the country-born is China's form of apartheid'.

Rural migrants are frequently distinguishable by the poor quality of their dress and by their size. Throughout their lives most have been less well fed than their urban counterparts. They are generally looked down upon by established urbanites and often poorly treated at work, even in the formal sector. In general they do the menial jobs that urbanites desperately try to avoid. Some can only find work in extremely dangerous occupations, for example hanging by a single rope to clean the windows of Beijing's colony of skyscrapers. The accident rate in this, and many other urban occupations is extremely high by western standards. Migrants are also subject to the arbitrary justice of the authorities. One example is a settlement on the outskirts of Beijing where some 50,000 migrants settled over the years to produce much of the capital's clothing. In 1996 a quasi-military operation involving nearly 5000 armed police and soldiers emptied the village and razed the buildings.

Rural to urban migration in China is reported negatively in both the Chinese and the international press. The concerns of urban planners, including the increased demands migrants place on housing, public utilities and transport, have been highlighted. Migrants are blamed for the rise in crime in urban areas. They are thought to lack the constraints of a bonding group and therefore act in anti-social ways. However, internal migration is not a new phenomenon in China. The country's population has never been sedentary, and there was significant migration before the 1949 Revolution. Indeed current migration streams seem to be built partly on this.

In a detailed study using migration data for the period 1982–87 (1% sampling population) Shen identified employment as the major cause of migration (Figure 18), accounting for nearly 30% of migrations. Marriage was the second major cause of movement, with migration to join family close behind. Marriage migration is female dominated. All other reasons were far less significant. In terms of age the 15–29 age group recorded the highest migration rates. In fact the 20–24 band accounted for over 30% of in-migrations of city populations. A much higher proportion, nearly 50% of in-migrants to rural areas were in the 20–24 age group, with marriage the most likely reason for most of these migrations.

In-migrants are generally more skilled than the total population. On average, the percentage of population with beyond primary school education is nearly 90% in the in-migrant population but less than 75% in the total population. In the in-migrant population over 8% have a university education while in the total population the proportion is only 1%.

In terms of the destination distribution of migrants Shen reached the following conclusions:

- Migrants from cities are most likely to move to other cities.
- Migrants from towns usually move to other towns at the intra-provincial level but to cities at the inter-provincial level.
- Migrants from the country (the rural population) invariably move to towns at the intra-provincial level and to cities at the inter-provincial level.
- Cities and towns have high in-migration rates while country populations have a low in-migration rate.
- Out-migration rates from cities, towns and rural areas are reasonably close, though the country population has the highest rates.
- Intra-provincial migration rates are higher than inter-provincial rates.
- City populations have a relatively higher inter-provincial rate than town and country populations.

A number of recent surveys indicate that rural labour migrants are predominantly male (between 70% and 85%). However, specific circumstances lead to higher female participation in some areas. In poor regions the participation of women is somewhat higher in less poor households. A study in Anhui showed that a local migration tradition caused an almost equal gender balance in migration. The mean age of internal migrants in China is estimated to be 31 years with 70–80% under 30 years of age. Female mobility decreases more rapidly than male movement with age. Marital status is more important for women than for men in determining rates of migration. The education level of rural migrants is on average higher than that of the total population. The proportion of migrants with some special skills is also higher than among the total population. The poorest areas do not usually have the highest rates of out-migration. People in these areas do not have access to the most rewarding activities in urban areas, though they may migrate to activities nearby, for seasonal agriculture and less rewarding work. The development of rural enterprises appears to increase rates of out-migration, except among the more educated peasants.

Roberts (1997) refers to Chinese migrants from Hunan province who earned between 100 and 200 yuan per month and remitted an average of 1000 yuan per year. He also reports results from a 1993 survey, according to which migrants earned an average of 3649 yuan during 205 days worked away from home, while the rural per capita income was 922 yuan. Little remittance money is invested in agriculture in comparison with family maintenance, improving housing, weddings and dowries.

A series of field studies centred on villages of migrant origin in the provinces of Jiangsu, Anhui, Sichuan and Gansu noted that high rates of out-migration are caused not only by land scarcity but also by rising costs of agriculture, and a strong desire of villagers to leave farming. In some cases labour shortages resulted. The conclusion regarding remittances was that although they might benefit individual families they do not contribute to village income and development nor to the establishment and maintenance of village services including those for facilitating agricultural development.

China currently has over 100 million surplus rural labourers and 5.2 million urban unemployed. Expanding township industries have already absorbed about 130 million rural labourers, but urban unemployment has been rising due to the closure of many state-run loss-making enterprises. It has been calculated that the labour force will increase by a further 30% in the next 25 years. Rapid economic growth will need to be sustained to absorb so many new workers. The growth of three metropolitan areas in particular could be potentially phenomenal. These are the Zhujiang delta region, the Changjiang delta region and the Beijing, Tianjin and Tangshan region. However, although the total number of people involved in rural to urban migration is massive in comparison to the rest of the world, it has to be placed in the context of a total population of over 1250 million. Indeed, the proportion of migrants to the total population is not very large by international standards.

Under China's next national Five Year Plan, due to begin in 2002, it is planned to move 300 million rural dwellers into 10,000 new towns. This policy is mainly the result of the government's failure to control the huge influx of poor peasants into the bulging cities. The construction of the new towns will result in the loss of millions of hectares of arable land. The scheme will entail spending an estimated £200 billion on housing and infrastructure development. Many of the people likely to be encompassed by the scheme are far from happy. Large scale protests are expected from those forced to leave rural homes to make way for the new towns. The environmental problems that such large scale construction will bring are also formidable.

Summary

- Migrations can be differentiated in terms of space, time, and motive.
- The causes of migration can be examined at three scales: macro-level, meso-level and micro-level.
- Migration is a selective process influenced by economic, social, cultural, political and environmental factors.
- The characteristics of migrants are crucial to the effect of migration on economic development in areas of origin and destination.
- Much recent research has concentrated on gender differences and family influences on migration.
- There is a range of theories regarding the importance of migrant remittances.
- The relationship between migration and development is complex and as yet imperfectly understood.
- The main policy approaches to migration can be classified as: negative, accommodative, manipulative and preventive.
- In absolute terms rural to urban migration in China is currently operating at an unprecedented scale.

Questions

1. Study Figure 11
   a What do you understand by the terms (i) counter-stream (ii) step migration?
   b Explain two possible reasons for rural to rural migration.
   c Discuss the relationship between the 'distance' and 'direction' components of migration.
   d Examine one aspect of migration that is not included in Figure 11?
   e For one LEDC you have studied, examine its human migration in terms of distance, direction and patterns.

2. Study Figure 15
   a Explain two reasons for rural to urban migration.
   b To what extent and why is rural to urban migration selective?
   c Discuss the 'support costs' flowing from village to city.
   d What are remittances? Suggest how remittances are used in rural areas.
   e Comment on the possible positive and negative effects of the other flows from city to village.
3. Study Figure 16
   a Why have a number of countries attempted to reduce the rate of internal migration in the post-1945 period?
   b Suggest two ways in which a negative policy approach could be implemented.
   c Discuss ways in which an accommodative approach could reduce the negative effects of migration.
   d Explain one planning measure that could be used to redirect migration flows towards alternative destinations (the manipulative approach).
   e Outline the merits and potential limitations of the preventive approach to migration.
4. Study Figure 17
   a Describe the projected changes to China's rural and urban populations to 2087.
   b Identify the main reasons for intra-provincial and inter-provincial migration in China.
   c Why has internal migration been of such concern to the Chinese government over the past 50 years?

5 Internal migration in the MEDCs

KEY WORDS

Rural depopulation: the decrease in population of rural areas, whether by falling birth rates or by migration as young people move away, usually to urban areas.

Counterurbanisation: the process of population decentralisation as people move from large urban areas to smaller urban settlements and rural areas.

Reurbanisation: when, after a clear period of decline, the population of a city, in particular the inner city, begins to increase again.

1 Introduction

Migration was a common part of the European economy before industrialisation. It was essential to the settlement of early medieval Europe and an integral part of early modern life in western Europe. According to Moch (1997) 'In the countrysides, regional migration routines were part of the agricultural cycle, family formation, and the supply of the rural labour force. Harvest work took thousands of men out of their own regions and in many cases across national borders. Migration to large and small cities provided an alternative to village life for young people and added newcomers to urban demographic systems which were chronically in deficit.'

Since the late eighteenth century two significant trends can be identified concerning the redistribution of population in MEDCs. The first, urbanisation, lasted until about 1970, while the second, counterurbanisation, has been dominant since that time. The process of urbanisation had a considerable impact on many rural areas where depopulation occurred because of it. Counterurbanisation, which has resulted in a renaissance in the demographic fortunes of rural areas is often referred to as the 'population turnaround'. There has been considerable debate as to whether this trend will be long term or relatively short-lived.

2 Urbanisation

a) The urban Industrial Revolution

The urban Industrial Revolution based on the introduction of mass production in factories commenced in Britain in the late eighteenth century. This was an era when industrialisation and urbanisation proceeded hand in hand. The key invention, among many, was the steam engine. The huge demand for labour in the rapidly growing coalfield towns and cities was satisfied by the freeing of labour in agriculture through a series of major advances. The so-called 'Agricultural Revolution' had in fact begun in the late seventeenth century.

By 1801 nearly one-tenth of the population of England and Wales was living in cities of over 100,000 people. This proportion doubled in 40 years and doubled again in another 60 years. However, at the global scale fewer than 3% of the population lived in urban areas at the beginning of the nineteenth century.

London, which had an estimated population of 575,000 in 1700 housed over one million people in 1801, according to the first census of England and Wales held that year. By 1851 London's population had more than doubled to over 2.5 million. The 1901 census put London's population at almost 6.6 million. The comparable figures for Birmingham were 71,000 in 1801, 233,000 in 1851, and 760,000 in 1901. As the processes of the Industrial Revolution spread to other countries the pace of urbanisation quickened. It took about 80 years for the urban population of England and Wales to increase from 10% to 30% of the total population. In the USA it took 66 years; in Germany 48 years; in Japan 36 years; and in Australia 26 years.

The transition from industrial capitalism to monopoly capitalism (Figure 19) marked the next stage of urbanisation in recent history. This transition was characterised by:

- a much greater scale of economic activity
- the consolidation of firms into multinational corporations
- the domination of newly created international markets by a small number of producers in each sector

	1780–1880	1880–1950	1950–
Mode of accumulation			
Economic formation	Industrial capitalism	Monopoly capitalism	Corporate capitalism
Source of wealth	Manufacturing	Manufacturing	Manufacturing and services
Representative unit	Factory	Multinational	Trans-national corporation,
of production		corporation	global factory
World-system characteristics			
Space relations	Atlantic basin	International	Global
System of supply	Colonialism/	State imperialism	Corporate imperialism
	imperialism	Britain, USA	USA
Hegemonic powers	Britain		
Urban consequences			
Level of urbanisation at	3	5	27
start of period (%)	Britain	North-western	Africa and Asia
Areas of urbanisation		Europe, the	
during period		Americas, coasts of	
		Empires	
Dominant cities	London	London, New York	New York, London, Tokyo

Figure 19 The principal stages in global urban development
Source: The Geographical Journal Vol. 164, No. 1, March 1998

- the mass production of a very much wider range of goods and services than previously
- the ruthless exploitation of peripheral areas.

Such a transition went hand in hand with further urbanisation in MEDCs while giving an initial impetus to urbanisation in LEDCs. The initial urbanisation of many LEDCs was restricted to concentrations of population around points of supply of raw materials for the affluent MEDCs. For example, the growth of Sao Paulo was firmly based on coffee, Buenos Aires on mutton, wool and cereals, and Calcutta on jute.

Today, around 75% of people in MEDCs live in urban areas, compared to only 38% in LEDCs as a whole. Tokyo remains the world's most heavily populated city with 27.2 million people, but of the world's ten largest cities only two more, New York and Los Angeles, are in the developed world.

b) Rural depopulation

Rural depopulation has affected all MEDCs to a greater or lesser extent in the late nineteenth and twentieth centuries. In England and Wales almost a third of all rural districts were still losing population in 1971 although since then the total area affected by this phenomenon has reduced significantly. Depopulation is now confined to extremely isolated parts of the country. Figure 20 is a simple model of the depopulation process which can have a considerable economic, social and demographic impact on the communities affected.

As threshold populations fall, services depart. The first to go are those in the private sector where delay can be financially fatal. Public

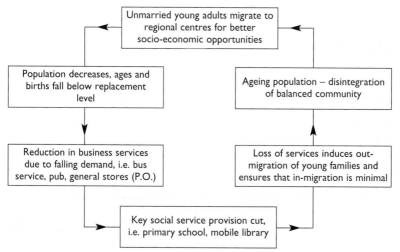

Figure 20 The downward spiral of rural depopulation

services may last longer but there is a limit to how long local governments can maintain services for small populations when there are so many demands on their finances. At each level of service decline the temptation to leave increases amongst those in the population for whom it is a viable option. There is a strong relationship between population size and service provision. For example in England, 59% of parishes with a population of under 1000 have no permanent shop of any kind compared with 1% for parishes with a population between 3000 and 9999, according to the 1997 Survey of Rural Services.

In the Republic of Ireland, one area that has suffered almost consistently from this problem is the Gaeltacht, the Irish-speaking districts of the West. After a lull in the 1970s compared to earlier years, the exodus of young people resumed in earnest in the early 1980s. One community severely affected by this trend was Lettermore, a group of islands off Galway, connected to the mainland by bridges. In 1987 alone, one sixth of Lettermore's population (then about 2500) emigrated. Most were young, and their departure made it impossible for local football and hurling clubs to assemble teams on a regular basis. Whole families were uprooted, abandoned cottages standing in the stony fields as evidence. Some villages were almost deserted. The strength of the Irish economy in the 1990s has slowed the out-migration of young people as well as attracting newcomers, often retirees from countries such as Holland and Germany who value the environmental attractions of the region. However, the problem for young people remains; it is difficult to attract large employers to the absolute periphery of Europe.

3 Counterurbanisation

According to Lewis (2000) 'counterurbanisation involves a series of fundamental changes in the redistribution of population including a population shift out of core industrial regions and into the peripheral regions as well as movements down the urban hierarchy'. Changes in telecommunications in particular have helped to diversify many non-metropolitan economies so that they are now viable locations for employers and residents in search of less congestion, lower costs and a better quality of life.

The general consensus is that population turnaround first became evident in the USA in the 1970s and that since then most countries of western Europe as well as Australia, New Zealand, Canada and Japan have followed suit. There is evidence to suggest that population growth was taking place on the fringe of British cities as early as the 1950s, from where it spread into more intermediate areas in the 1960s and then, during the 1970s, to the rural periphery. Thus, it seems the starting point of counterurbanisation was the transformation of the most accessible rural settlements within the metropolitan hinterland into commuter communities. As a 'rural' lifestyle became more popular amongst urbanites its spatial impact gradually diffused into more remote regions.

In all the countries affected, the movement of urbanites into rural areas has reduced differences in culture, lifestyle and population composition. There has been much debate about the causes of counterurbanisation. The most plausible explanations are as follows:

- The 'period' explanation emphasises the role of the peculiar economic and demographic circumstances of the 1970s. The energy crisis, periods of recession, the sharp growth in retirees and the impact of the post-war baby boom combined to weaken metropolitan growth. In metropolitan areas push factors had never been stronger while, perhaps for the first time, rural location was a viable alternative for many. This perspective viewed counterurbanisation as a very temporary phenomenon which would subside once economic and demographic conditions returned to 'normal'.
- The 'regional restructuring' explanation emphasises the role of the new organisation of production, the changing spatial division of labour and the increasing importance of service industries. All these factors stimulated a greater spread of activities and population towards smaller places and the rural periphery.
- The 'de-concentration' explanation highlights the lowering of institutional and technological barriers to rural location. Long-standing preferences for lower density environments are now much less constrained than in the past and an increasing number of businesses and households have felt free to leave the metropolitan areas, confident that their prospects will improve rather than diminish. The key factor here is the convergence, across size and place, in the availability of amenities that were previously accessible only in larger places.

A detailed examination of the demographic balance between metropolitan and non-metropolitan areas in MEDCs since 1970 shows that not all countries have behaved in the same way. In the 1970s counterurbanisation was clearly evident in virtually all MEDCs, although some rural regions in most countries continued to lose population. However, in the 1980s a number of countries, notably the USA, Canada, Ireland and Australia showed a demographic reversal with metropolitan areas experiencing net inflows. For example, during the 1980s metropolitan areas in the USA experienced net migration gains of 4% while the non-metropolitan areas had net losses of about 3%. In MEDCs which did not experience a reversal in favour of metropolitan areas the demographic turnaround slowed down. This was certainly the case in England and Wales where, for example, Greater London halved its rate of population loss compared to the 1970s. The non-metropolitan districts in England and Wales continued to increase their populations but at a reduced rate with the 'remoter, mainly rural districts' showing the fastest rates of growth at this time. However, by the early 1990s the reversal recorded in the previous decade in a number of countries had given way to another revival in the demographic fortunes of the countryside.

Thus, over the last three decades the pattern of population redistribution in the developed world has been:

- Population decline in metropolitan areas and significant growth in non-metropolitan regions in the 1970s.
- A reversal in the 1980s in some countries which experienced metropolitan growth. Other countries experienced a slower rate of non-metropolitan growth compared to the 1970s.
- A general return to universal counterurbanisation in the 1990s.

Lewis (2000) argues that if we are to accurately assess the impact of counterurbanisation we have to look beyond actual numbers and focus on the selectivity of migrants within the context of household turnover, 'At a regional level it is now realised that net migration provides only a partial picture of the process of social change since net migration gains or losses are only the surface ripples of powerful cross-currents'. It has been clear for some time now that the growth in the number of households in Britain is at a much higher level than the growth in population. On the basis of household change, the demographic turnaround of the 1970s was much more powerful than that revealed by population change alone. Stated at the most basic level, the in-migration of 200 people into a rural area today, means more new houses than it would have done in 1950 when people lived in larger households. However, it is not just numbers but also the socio-economic characteristics of the people involved. Even in regions where counterurbanisation is very pronounced, people still leave rural communities. For example, the selective out-migration of the young continues for the same reasons as in the past. When those who move in differ in their socio-economic characteristics from those they replace, what may be termed 'replacement selectivity', then social re-composition takes place.

4 Internal and international migration

In a number of MEDCs there is a sharp contrast between the destinations of immigrants and domestic migrants. In 1995, 94% of new immigrants to the USA settled in metropolitan areas, with 46% selecting just 10 metropolitan areas as their destinations. The populations of many large cities have been substantially altered by immigration in recent decades. For example, the 1990 Census showed that 38% of Los Angeles' population, 28% of New York's population and 17% of Chicago's population were foreign born. The US metropolitan areas that gain the most from domestic migrants show relatively small gains from immigration, and on the whole they are much further down the settlement hierarchy. Whites now account for less than 60% of the population of the 25 biggest metropolitan areas but 147 out of

America's 271 metropolitan areas are at least 80% white. Thus, the major city focus of immigrants is as strong as ever at a time when an increasing number of native-born whites, many of them at the middle and lower income levels, are moving out of large metropolitan areas to communities lower down the settlement hierarchy. A key area of recent research has been to examine the link between the two trends.

This element of domestic migration has been viewed by some as a viable alternative to further suburbanisation. It represents a response to growing employment opportunities in less costly environments as well as severe pressure on the wages of the relatively unskilled caused by a high inflow of immigrants. This out-migration has occurred in both economic booms and busts over the past few decades, and it is significant for both inner city and suburban regions. The contribution of this group to nonmetropolitan growth contrasts sharply with the stereotypic characterisations of urban to rural migrants: self-employed professionals who move to high amenity locations and telecommunicate with their clients; the footloose retiree population; or 'return migrant' urban Blacks to family or birthplace origins in the rural South. Demographically these domestic migrants have more in common with local intra-suburban movers, despite the fact that they are leaving the metropolitan area entirely. Some observers have suggested that the current movement is a new, more dispersed form of the old suburban 'White flight' although others have argued strongly against the use of such terminology. Nevertheless, it is clear that the characteristics of the current migrant population resemble, to a large degree, the population that participated in the movement from inner cities to suburbs in the 1950s and 1960s. This movement sharpened the demographic gap between inner city and suburb with respect to race-ethnicity and the current movement out of metropolitan areas has the potential to do the same. It is clear that the rural renaissance of the 1990s is very much a domestic migration phenomenon.

Case Study: Internal migration in Britain

a) Population distribution before the Industrial Revolution

Although many population movements had occurred in Britain prior to the Industrial Revolution, it was this event that set in motion the greatest redistribution of people in the history of the country. In England 80% of the population in 1770 was rural; in 1850 the balance between town and country was even; by 1931 only 20% of the population was recorded as living in rural districts.

Before the Industrial Revolution, the distribution of population in Britain reflected the agricultural value of land. Prior to 1750 the most densely peopled region was a broad belt of country stretching from the Wash to the Severn estuary. London and its immediate environs, with 0.75 million people, lay almost in the middle of the southern edge of this belt. To the south and east of it, large tracts of forest ensured a lower population density, while to the north and west, even in the lowlands, population thinned rapidly. The uplands and the highlands were inhabited by very few people indeed. This was the pattern reconstructed by economic historians and demographers from taxation returns and parish registers, and checked by calculations from later census figures.

Although the majority of the population had always been engaged in agriculture, as time passed industry occupied an increasing number of people. But even in 1750 industry was widely dispersed, broadly related to the fertility of the soil. This was true not only for industries such as milling, malting, leather working, the building of carts, wagons, carriages, coaches and ships, but also of the two major industries, iron working and textile manufacture. Specialisation was easiest and local markets largest where population density was high. However, this is not to deny the existence of some industry where soil was infertile, where people sought to make the living denied to them by the land.

b) 1750 to 1851

By 1801, the year of the first census, change was apparent and by the middle of the nineteenth century the regional distribution of population had changed considerably. High population density reflected industrial activity and the accessibility of coal. A succession of inventions, in the eighteenth and nineteenth centuries, with the steam engine at the forefront, revolutionised industry and brought into being agglomerations of factories on or near the coalfields. Improvements in transport made it possible to bring together in one place large quantities of food and raw materials and to distribute the products of industry far and wide.

During the first half of the nineteenth century the increase in population characteristic of Stage 2 of demographic transition, affected the countryside as well as the towns. In fact death rates in rural Britain fell faster than in the towns due to poor housing and lack of adequate sanitation in the latter. Urban population grew mainly by migration from the countryside rather than by natural increase. Due to this movement the rural population grew less rapidly than in urban areas. It was not just the growing demand for labour in the towns and cities but also agricultural change that fuelled the large scale movement of people from rural areas. New machinery had reduced the labour requirement on many farms, while increasing imports of foreign wheat caused many farmers, especially on the heavier soils of the wetter West to change from arable farming to grass with its lower labour requirement. However, during this period, Acts of Enclosure (labour required for hedging), reclamation schemes and the more intensive use of farmland actually increased rural population in some areas and kept it stable in others.

c) 1851 to 1911

In the second half of the nineteenth century many rural areas experienced prolonged and significant depopulation (Figure 21). The demand for labour for hedging and draining declined and the march of mechanisation continued. Ironically, after 1870 when rural depopulation reached particularly high levels, more mechanisation was called for to combat labour shortages. Rural based trades and professions also declined as urban products and services gained increasing market share in the countryside. The decline in this sector of rural life proved to be a further stimulus

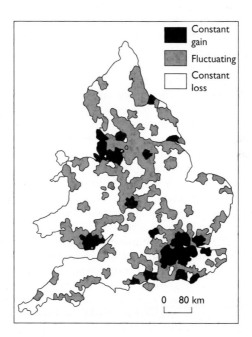

Figure 21 Migrational change in England and Wales, 1851–1911
Source: Population Geography, Hornby & Jones, CUP, 1993

to out-migration for those who remained. It was during this period that the contrast between urban growth and rural decline was at its greatest.

The 1911 Census of England and Wales showed that, for the first time farmers and farm workers were no longer the single largest occupational group, having been surpassed by miners and metal workers. Between 1861 and 1911 the number of agricultural labourers (including shepherds) over the age of 20 fell from 809,000 to 498,000. During the same period the total rural population dropped from 9.1 million to 7.9 million. In proportional terms this was a decline from 45.4% of the total population to 21.9%. The main destinations of these rural migrants were London, the fast growing coalfield industrial towns (especially in South Wales, the West Midlands, South Lancashire, West and South Yorkshire, Northumberland and Durham) and the ports of Humberside and Merseyside. Between 1851 and 1911 the urban population rose from 9 million to almost 28 million. The majority of in-migrants to urban areas were young and the rapid increase in the urban population was the result of both in-migration and high birth rates.

d) 1911 to 1951

Between 1911 and 1951 the process of rural depopulation continued in the remotest and most agricultural of the rural areas. Net migration losses occurred in Exmoor, central Wales, Norfolk, the Fens, large parts of Lincolnshire, the Vale of Pickering, the North York Moors and the northern Pennines. However, at the same time the conurbations and the coalfield industrial towns also experienced net out-migration although this tended to be more than offset by natural increase. Movement from the conurbations was partly spontaneous and partly planned. An increasing number of people wanted the advantages of rural residence while continuing to work in the city. Rural areas were now perceived to provide a better quality of life compared with the pollution, congestion and other negative externalities of the cities.

Alongside this was the planned rehousing of communities from inner-city slums. Because of the lack of space in the cities themselves many new council estates were constructed at urban margins and in rural areas within commuting distance. Out-migration from the coalfields was due to the stagnation or decline of the heavy industries of the industrial revolution. Coalmining, shipbuilding, heavy engineering and textiles all recorded sharp falls in employment as Britain lost many of its traditional markets in the face of foreign competition. The lack of diversification in many industrial towns often meant that a new job could only be found elsewhere, and an increasing number of people adopted this option. Early attempts at regional policy such as the 1934 Special Areas Act which assisted the North-East, South Wales and West Cumberland helped to reduce out-migration to a degree but its impact was not strong enough to halt the process.

The positive industry mix of the South East and the Midlands due to the influx of new technology industries such as motor vehicles, electrical engineering and aircraft manufacture was in marked contrast to the negative industry mix of the heavy industrial regions. In addition, key service industries were overwhelmingly concentrated in the South East. The contrast between the dynamic South and industrial decline in the North could not have been much greater. The resultant 'drift to the South' was not difficult to predict.

Two interesting developments during this period were the growth of retirement regions, in rural as well as urban locations in the coastal areas of Cornwall, Devon, Hampshire, Sussex, Kent, North Wales and Lancashire, as well as net migration gains in rural coalfield areas where deep, concealed coal measures were being exploited for the first time.

e) 1951 to 1971

In this 20 year period the most remote Welsh counties and the most northerly English rural counties continued to suffer migration losses. Thus, rural depopulation was now affecting a much more restricted geographical area. The conurbations and largest cities continued to lose population as did the old industrial regions of northern England and South Wales. During this time the Assisted Areas benefited from a relatively high level of funding and the various measures employed in promoting industrial development undoubtedly slowed down out-migration. Nevertheless, out-migration, along with most other indicators of socio-economic concern was above the national average in Assisted Areas in the 1950s and 1960s.

Another arm of government policy which had a significant effect on internal migration was the construction of New Towns, initiated by the New Towns Act of 1946 (Figure 22). 14 New Towns were designated between 1946 and 1950 with only one, Cumbernauld in Scotland, added in the 1950s. These are regarded as the first generation New Towns which were largely mechanisms for replacing bomb-damaged houses and reducing the extremely high population densities in the inner areas of London and Glasgow. However, a few New Towns such as

Figure 22 Crawley New Town has proved to be an attractive
location for both industry and population

Cwmbran in South Wales were intended to act primarily as small
growth poles in the commercially depressed Assisted Areas. Later
New Towns, the so-called second generation, such as
Washington on Tyneside were seen primarily as new economic
growth poles which would bring prosperity to traditional industrial areas. Last of all came the 'New Cities' or third generation
New Towns of Milton Keynes, Telford and Central Lancashire
which were planned to be larger than their earlier counterparts
and act as 'counter magnets' to people who might otherwise
have moved to London. By 1976 32 New Towns had been designated in Britain.

The planned relocation of urban populations combined with
voluntary out-migration in search of a better lifestyle resulted in
a marked decentralisation of population from the large urban
areas, particularly between 1961 and 1971. The only conurbation
to record a population increase in the 1960s was West Yorkshire,
an urban area with no related New Towns.

Population growth was greatest in the area south of a line
from the Wash to the mouth of the Severn. In this area the counties nearest to London grew most rapidly in the 1950s whereas in

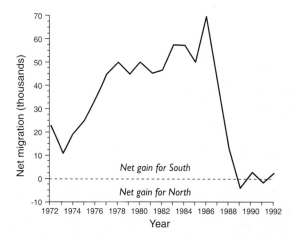

Figure 23 Population gains for the South of England
Source: The Population of Britain in the 1990s, T. Champion *et al.*
Clarendon Press, Oxford (1996)

the 1960s they recorded lower rates of growth than counties in the outer parts of the region. This was the result of the gradual outward diffusion of planned and voluntary population and industrial decentralisation.

f) Migration since 1971

At the regional scale the level of net gains for the South rose steeply during the mid-1970s to around 50,000 a year (Figure 23). However, between 1986 and 1988 the relative attractiveness of the South dropped dramatically as it was a time of major economic depression which had a much more severe impact on the South than earlier periods of economic downturn. However, as the economy recovered the drift to the South resumed once more.

A reasonable question to ask is why the movement from high unemployment areas in the North and West to the South has not been greater. The answer is that the unemployed are one of the least mobile groups in society and they invariably lack the appropriate skills in demand in the new sectors of the economy. In addition they often face insurmountable problems in terms of finding affordable accommodation along with a reluctance to leave family and community. All these factors mitigate against a free flow of labour within the British economy.

The South East can be seen as an 'escalator' region, providing opportunities for advancement for young adults. But later in the life cycle, due to promotion, business ownership, self-employment or simply a better quality of life, many move out of the region. Growth regions tend to attract a disproportionate share of young adults, and locations which are losing such people become unbalanced in their population structure. The inflow into the South East is being matched by a counter-current of migration from the metropolitan core into East Anglia and parts of the South West in particular. The population of the South West increased from 3.7 million in 1961 to 4.8 million in 1994. However, only part of this expansion can be accounted for by 'overspill' from the South East; it also reflects a growing popularity of the region for retirement migration and the success of local economies in places such as Bristol and Bournemouth.

As in the South West, population growth in East Anglia is only partly accounted for by overspill. It has also been the result of strong economic growth in key urban centres as well as the expansion of East Anglian ports with increasing European trade.

In recent years British cities have, to a limited extent, reversed the population decline that has dominated the last half a century. In fact Merseyside was the only urban region whose population fell between 1991 and 1996. Central government finance, for example the millions of pounds of subsidies poured into

				Thousands		
	Within the UK			International[2]		
	To	From	Net	To	From	Net
0–15	16.1	36.8	−20.7	7.2	4.7	2.5
16–24	66.1	4.50	21.1	38.1	9.6	28.5
25–44	70.3	92.0	−21.7	35.9	34.5	1.4
45–64	11.0	27.2	−16.2	3.3	3.9	−0.5
65+	5.1	16.4	−11.3	0.4	−	0.4
All ages	168.5	217.4	−48.9	84.8	52.7	32.1

1 Mid-1996 to mid-1997.
2 Excludes asylum seekers/visitor switchers and movements to and from the Irish Republic.

Figure 24 Migration to and from London (by age, 1996–7)[1]
Source: Focus on London 99 – a joint publication from the Government Statistical Service, the Government Office for London and the London Research Centre, 1999

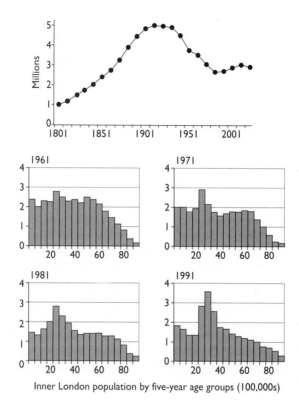

Figure 25 Population change and age structure in inner London
Source: AS Geography: Concepts and Cases, P. Guinness & G. Nagle,
Hodder & Stoughton, 2000

London's Docklands, Manchester's Hulme wastelands and
Sheffield's light railway, has been an important factor in the
revival. New urban design is also playing a role and the reduction
in urban street crime due to the installation of automated closed-
curcuit surveillance cameras has significantly improved public
perception of central areas.

Is the recent reurbanisation just a short term blip or the
beginning of a significant trend at least in the medium term?
Perhaps the most important factor favouring the latter is the government's prediction of the formation of 4.4 million extra
households over the next two decades. 60% of these new households will have to be housed in existing urban areas because
there is such fierce opposition to the relaxation of planning
restrictions in the countryside.

London

The levels of net migration affecting London are the sum of separate estimates for movements within Britain and international migration. In the 1980s the average annual net migration loss was about 16,000. In contrast in the 1990s there has been a small annual average increase. Since 1991 London's annual net migration loss to the rest of Britain, as measured by the National Health Service Central Register has fluctuated around 50,000. In 1997 it was 49,000 (Figure 24). However, the annual losses mask a consistently large inflow of young adults. London has had net migrational gains from most regions in Britain since 1994. But because of large losses to the South East and Eastern regions, overall net migration has been negative. 60–65% of those leaving London have destinations in the South East or Eastern regions.

Perhaps the most surprising aspect in the turnaround of London's population is the rejuvenation of inner London where the population peaked at 5 million in 1900 but then steadily dropped to a low of 2.5 million by 1983. The Department of the Environment forecasts it will reach 3 million by 2011. This change in the fortunes of inner London has had a significant impact on population structure (Figure 25) with a considerable increase in the young adult age groups. The economic impact of this influx of young adults should not be underestimated, as migrants, both internal and international, tend to be the more imaginative and enterprising of their peers.

Summary

- Migration was a common phenomenon in pre-industrial Europe and other MEDCs.
- Before the Industrial Revolution the distribution of population was largely related to the fertility of the land.
- The rapid development of industry on the coalfields and at nearby ports during the Industrial Revolution 'pulled' a large amount of labour to the expanding urban areas.
- At the same time improvements in agriculture reduced the demand for labour in most rural areas. The lack of alternative opportunities 'pushed' the unemployed and underemployed to seek new jobs in the industrial towns.
- In the first half of the nineteenth century out-migration caused rural areas to grow less rapidly than urban areas. In the latter half of the nineteenth century out-migration resulted in rural depopulation in many rural areas.
- Depopulation continued to affect the most remote and the most agricul-

tural parts of Britain in the first half of the twentieth century. In the latter part of the century the geographical area affected by depopulation shrank.

- The 'drift to the South' has been virtually relentless in the post Second World War period.
- Since the beginning of the 1970s counterurbanisation has been a very significant process in all MEDCs.
- In recent years the phenomenon of reurbanisation has been recognised but it is too early to say if this is a long term process.

Questions

1. Study Figure 20
   a Define the terms (i) rural depopulation and (ii) replacement level.
   b Why is out-migration from rural areas dominated by young adults?
   c Suggest reasons why privately owned services usually close in rural areas before publicly owned services.
   d Explain the impact of cuts in service provision.
   e How might local or regional government try to reverse such a trend?
   f For one named region explain why the cycle of rural depopulation began.

2. Study Figure 25
   a Describe the change in the population of inner London from 1801 onwards.
   b Suggest reasons for the changes you have described.
   c To what extent and why did the age distribution of inner London's population change from 1961 to 1991?
   d Discuss the likely impact of such changes in population structure on inner London.

6 International migration

1 Introduction

International migration is thought to be running at its highest rate ever despite increasingly tough measures against illegal immigration in both the USA and Europe. It has been estimated that over 125 million people lived outside their country of birth or citizenship at the end of the twentieth century. Accounting for about 2% of the world's population, the number of people involved is expanding annually.

2 Changing attitudes to immigration

A number of distinct periods can be recognised in terms of the attitudes of governments to immigration. Prior to 1914 government controls on international migration were almost non-existent. Except for a few countries such as Japan, states placed no serious constraints on the movement of people across their borders. For example, the USA allowed the entry of anybody who was not a prostitute, a convict, a lunatic and, after 1882, Chinese. Within Europe movement was largely uncontrolled with no requirement for passports or work permits. Foreign-born criminals could expect deportation, but that was the extent of immigration policy. Thus, the main obstacles to international movement at the time were cost and the physical dangers that might be associated with the journey.

Partly reflecting security concerns, international movement was curtailed between 1914 and 1945. During this period many countries pursued immigration policies which would now be classed as overtly racist. For example, in the USA Congress passed laws aiming to preserve the country's racial and religious composition. The early attempts made to control movements in Europe were aimed at preventing departures, especially of people with acquired skills.

According to Torpey (2000) 'The creation of the modern passport system, and the use of similar systems in the interior of a variety of countries ... signalled the dawn of a new era in human affairs, in which individual states and the international state system as a whole successfully monopolised the legitimate authority to permit movement within and across their jurisdictions'.

After 1945 many European countries, facing labour shortages, encouraged migrants from abroad. Initially the majority of workers came as temporary migrants from the poorer regions of Mediterranean Europe under bilateral labour recruitment agreements. However, increased economic growth caused several countries to look further afield. For some, former colonies were an obvious source. The Caribbean and South Asia were major sources of labour for Britain during this period while France looked to North and West Africa. The former West Germany attracted 'Gastarbeiter' or 'guest workers' from many countries but particularly from Turkey.

In the 1970s slow economic growth and rising unemployment in MEDCs led to a tightening of policy which, has remained in force. In the then EEC, legislation introduced in November 1973 placed severe restrictions on the movement of non-EEC workers into the member states. In a number of countries there was a strong backlash against immigrant communities. In 1973 Algeria suspended all emigration to France after 32 Algerians were murdered in France that year. As the industrialised nations made immigration more difficult in the wake of the 1973 oil crisis, the oil-rich countries of the Middle East opened the door to migrant workers as they needed extra labour to maximise the use of their increased petroleum revenues.

However, in some countries immigration did increase again in the 1980s and 1990s, spurring the introduction of new restrictions. Almost any country that has prospered relative to its neighbours has found that one consequence of success is increasing immigration pressure.

Immigration has also become increasingly difficult in LEDCs, for example in the relatively rich eastern Asian countries and South Africa. Opinion in South Africa has turned strongly against newcomers in recent years. The 'Malawian' newspaper reported Thabo Mbeki as saying 'Our people are just loafing in the streets at the expense of foreigners flooding our offices and mines. The Home Affairs Ministry will have to sort this thing out ... I mean these foreigners have got to go back home'. In West Africa migration opportunities changed significantly with the expulsion of between 200,000 and 1.5 million from Ghana in 1969, the expulsion of 2 million illegal 'aliens' from Nigeria in 1983, and increasing xenophobic attitudes in Ivory Coast. The attitudes of governments and the native-born populations of these and other countries to immigrants are influenced by a number of factors but in particular by the level of competition for employment. If the perception is that opportunities are being denied to the native-born, attitudes to newcomers can quickly change from tolerance to hostility.

3 The costs and benefits of international migration

Much has been written about the impact of international migration on donor and receiving countries in economic, social, demographic and political terms. From the literature available it is clear that the effects of immigration and emigration can vary significantly between nations. Migrants are often welcomed when times are good and their labour is needed but shunned when times are hard.

Figure 26, produced by the Organisation for Economic Co-operation and Development (OECD) provides a useful framework for the debate. It is interesting to note how many of the factors included in the table are labelled as having uncertain effects, as research in different countries often produces contradictory conclusions. In terms of economic impact on individual countries the data available are often insufficient to reach

	Benefits		Costs	
	Individual	Social	Individual	Social
Emigrant countries	1 Increased earning and employment opportunities 2* Training (human capital) 3* Exposure to new culture, etc.	1* Increased human capital with return migrants 2 Foreign exchange for investment via migrant remittances 3 Increased output per head due to outflow of unemployed and underemployed labour 4 Reduced pressure on public capital stock	1 Transport costs 2 Adjustment costs abroad 3 Separation from relatives and friends	1 Loss of social investment in education 2 Loss of 'cream' of domestic labour force 3* Social tensions due to raised expectations of return migrants 4* Remittances generate inflation by easing pressure on financing public sector deficits
Immigrant countries	1 (*) Cultural exposure, etc.	1 Permits growth with lower inflation 2 Increased labour force mobility and lower unit labour costs 3 Rise in output per head for indigenous workers	1 Greater labour market competition in certain sectors	1* Dependence on foreign labour in particular occupations 2 Increased demands on the public capital stock 3* Social tension with concentration of migrants in urban areas

* indicates uncertain effects

Figure 26 Short term costs and benefits of migration
Source: The Economist, 15 November 1988

firm conclusions and the social impact of immigration may be open to a wide range of interpretations. It must be remembered that each migration situation is unique. For some donor countries a migration that might provide a vital safety valve by relieving pressure on food supply and other resources may for other countries drastically reduce their future prospects by skimming off the skilled element of their labour supply. The impact on donor countries can also vary. Historically, emigration from the Republic of Ireland has been perceived as generally beneficial to the public purse by reducing unemployment and under-employment but its effect on the Gaeltacht, the isolated Irish-speaking regions of the West has been severe as so many have left over the years.

However, a number of general statements can be made without too much fear of contradiction:

- **Economic impact**: the general consensus among researchers is that immigration has improved the economic welfare of receiving countries. This is perhaps not surprising given the restrictive nature of immigration policies whereby receiving countries try to allow in only people with skills for which there is an excess demand in the labour market. Immigrants may develop new industries which can be of considerable benefit to the economy. Where immigrants are unskilled they usually do the jobs that the host population shuns. Most research contradicts the popular belief that immigration contributes to unemployment. The economic standing of immigrant groups tends to improve from generation to generation.
- **Social impact**: social assimilation usually follows on the back of economic assimilation, although the speed and degree to which it is achieved tends to be strongly related to the socio-political maturity of the host society as well as to the degree of difference between an immigrant community and the host society. Racial differences create the greatest barrier to social assimi-lation but differences in language, religion and culture can also be import-ant. As social barriers decline the benefits that different cultures can bring to society as a whole become more apparent. One of the great attractions of cities such as London and New York is their multiculturalism. The social impact on the donor country can also be considerable. This tends to occur in two stages. The first being the initial loss of many of its most dynamic indi-viduals. The second stage occurs as new ideas from the adopted country filter back to the home country, often clashing with traditional values.
- **Demographic impact**: as migration is selective there is invariably a sig-nificant impact on the population structures of both donor and receiving countries. International migration is frequently male dominated although less so now than in the past and it is also biased towards the younger age groups in the working population. Thus, its main effect is to slow down demographic ageing in the receiving country. As most migrants are in the reproductive age groups, if their numbers are sufficient they can reduce a declining birth rate or even cause it to increase. However, over time the demographic characteristics of most immigrant groups gradually move towards those of the country as a whole. This process invariably

begins when male migrants send for their families to join them. Conversely emigration reduces the working population and the birth rate of the donor countries. Emigration from rural districts in LEDCs, if it is large enough in scale, may result in demographic ageing and depopulation.

- **Political impact**: it can often take a considerable amount of time for immigrant communities to assimilate politically. Traditionally, immigrant voters have been drawn towards political parties which appear less nationalistic in outlook and more sympathetic to their concerns. Thus, in Britain the Labour Party attracts more voters from immigrant communities than the Conservatives while in the USA the Democrats benefit more than the Republicans from the immigrant vote. Living within a new political system can also affect the attitudes of immigrant communities as to what goes on back in their home country. The harshest critics of authoritarian governments in the Middle East and Asia are invariably exiles living in other countries.

Migrant culture, remittances and returnees

Migration does not only benefit those that take part in the process but also, through remittances, family and others left behind. However, due to cultural and other factors the importance of remittances varies considerably. It has been estimated that in the mid-1990s the global figure for remittances sent home by international migrants exceeded $75 billion a year, about twice the amount of official direct aid.

Mountz and Wright (1966) presented an interesting ethnographic account of the transnational migrant community of San Agustin, a village in the Mexican state of Oaxaca, and Poughkeepsie, a city in New York state. The link between the two communities began with the migration of a lone Oaxacan to Poughkeepsie in the early 1980s. In classic network fashion the Mexican population of Poughkeepsie, predominantly male, grew to well over 1000 over the next decade. Most Oaxacans found employment as undocumented workers in hotels, restaurants, shops and as building workers and landscapers. Their remittances transformed village life in their home community.

What struck Mountz and Wright most was the high level of connectedness between San Agustin and Poughkeepsie with the migrant community keeping in daily contact with family and friends via telephone, fax, camcorders, videotape and VCRs; communications technology that was rapidly being introduced to San Agustin. Rapid migration between the two communities was facilitated by jet travel and systems of wiring payments. In effect the community of San Agustin had been geographically extended to encompass the Oaxacan enclave in Poughkeepsie. This is a classic example of *time-space distanciation* – the stretching of social systems across space and time.

Migrant remittances were used not only to support the basic needs of families but also for home construction, the purchase of consumer goods and financing fiestas. The latter provided an important opportunity for migrants to display continued village membership.

However, as out-migration became more established tensions began to develop between some migrants and the home community. The main point of conflict was over the traditional system of communal welfare that requires males to provide service and support to the village. Where this could not be done in terms of time, a payment could be substituted. This was increasingly resented by some migrants who saw 'their money as their own'. However, this was not the only way that traditional village structures were coming under threat. Mountz and Wright identified six groups of people who were challenging traditional village atttitudes: dissenters 'los irresponsables', female migrants, Seventh Day Adventists, and Wife robbers (elopement). The traditionalists in the village cited migration as the major cause of the decline of established values and attitudes.

The researchers found that a migrant culture had now become established in San Agustin, as it had in so many other Mexican communities, for four main reasons:

- economic survival
- rite of passage for young male adults
- the growing taste for consumer goods and modern styles of living
- the enhanced status enjoyed by migrants in the home community.

In a study of Tongans and Samoans in Australia, Ahlbury and Brown found that those who planned to return home sent more money back than those who did not. The commitment to home rests upon complex emotional and social foundations. For those intending to return, it is undoubtedly advantageous to create a stock of socio-political capital on which they can draw upon return. The main conclusions drawn from this study were that:

- Only 10% of migrants intended to return home at some future date.
- There was no significant relationship between education and employment skills on the one hand and the intention to return home on the other.
- There was no indication that migrants near retirement age, or those already retired are more likely to return.
- It could be argued that the most desirable economic scenario is one in which all migrants keep alive the intention of returning without ever doing so.

Studies in the 1980s and 1990s of return migration have cast considerable doubt on the economic benefits to be gained from this process. Greenwood and Stuart (1986) have argued that it is not clear how migrants with low skill levels can be transformed into skilled workers by a period of employment overseas. Reichert and Massey (1982) have noted that even if such skills could be acquired, it is not clear that they are acquired. Rogers (1990) points out that return has very little impact when migrants return to their previous occupations or to retire. Borjas (1989), in a study of foreigners born in the USA, found that return migration is more likely among immigrants who did not perform well in the labour market. As Straubhaar (1986) concludes, it is not necessarily true that even if migrants acquire skills that they apply these skills upon returning home.

4 Global migrations

a) South Africa: Immigration and emigration

South Africa has a long history of immigration. For example, Dutch colonists imported Malay slaves to ease a labour shortage in the 1650s, and the country has relied on foreign workers, to a greater or lesser extent, ever since. Under the apartheid regime the government did not like letting more blacks into the country but found that foreigners could be exploited more easily than the domestic population which was often unionised. Since the end of White Rule in 1994 a new wave of migrants has been attracted to Africa's largest economy. Estimates for the number of undocumented migrants in South Africa range from 2 million to 8 million. South Africa's borders are long and porous and immigration laws are applied inconsistently across the country. Each year South Africa expels around 100,000 Mozambicans, but many find their way back without too much effort.

Many employers see immigration as essential to the well-being of the economy. In general migrant workers are prepared to work for lower wages than South Africans. They are less likely to be unionised and they have a reputation for working harder than the domestic population. They are often better educated too. Some industries rely very heavily on migrant labour. For example, South Africa's mines employ about 120,000 foreign workers, mainly from Mozambique and Lesotho. Farmers too rely to a considerable extent on foreign workers. However, migrants are also well represented in the service sector particularly in finance, education and health.

While employers value migrant labour, the government and many South Africans, particularly the less skilled are not so keen. The home-affairs minister Mangosuthu Buthelezi was recently quoted as saying 'the presence of illegal aliens impacts on housing, health services, education, crime, drugs, transmissible diseases – need I go on?' (The Economist, 2/9/2000). The general view that migrants are a burden on public services is not well supported by the evidence. According to a survey by the Southern African Migration Project (SAMP), only one fifth of migrant workers want to stay in South Africa permanently. This is not surprising as most migrate on an individual basis, leaving their dependants back in their home countries.

Impartial observers are virtually unanimous that migrant labour has significant economic benefits for South Africa but the net benefit has proved very difficult to quantify. Apart from the attributes discussed above, the role of migrant traders should also be considered. They often bring goods into South Africa which are not available locally. One study found that 78% of foreign traders selling goods in South Africa also purchased South African goods to sell in their own country. In addition, a significant proportion of migrant remittances are in the form of goods as opposed to cash. This is because few migrant workers have bank accounts and the quality and range of goods in South African shops is generally much better than in their own countries.

Migrant remittances are important to the economies of neighbouring countries. In Lesotho, miners' remittances account for almost one tenth of GDP. In southern Mozambique, almost three-quarters of respondents to a SAMP survey said that a family member was working in South Africa. Among those who had been to South Africa themselves, 87% had saved enough to buy a house.

However, migration is not all one way. The University of Cape Town estimates that 233,000 South Africans emigrated permanently between 1989 and 1997. Most were skilled people with few legal immigrants arriving to take their place (just over 4000 in 1998). Perhaps alarming for the government a SAMP survey in 2000 found that skilled black South Africans were almost as likely to consider emigrating as whites.

b) Immigration into the European Union

Large scale immigration into western Europe is a relatively recent phenomenon. Between 1960 and 1973 the number of foreign workers in the region doubled from 3% to 6% of the workforce. It was highest in countries like France and Britain which gave citizens of their former colonies relatively open access. In Germany too, the number of foreigners rose rapidly during this period although the 'guest workers' seldom became citizens. Although *primary immigration* into Europe, driven by labour shortages, all but ended with the oil crisis of 1973, the foreign-born population has continued to grow because:

- Most EU countries issue significant numbers of residence permits each year for the purposes of family reunification. For example, nearly 80% of the 58,700 people accepted for permanent settlement in Britain in 1997 were wives and children.
- Work permits are also issued in considerable numbers within the EU. In Britain in 1997, nearly half of the 54,000 permits went to Americans and Japanese, mainly in highly skilled jobs.
- The number of people applying for asylum has risen sharply since the late 1980s. In 1984 there were only 104,000 applications in western Europe. This figure rose to 692,000 in 1992 and then declined during much of the 1990s. Applications rose again in 1998, to 350,000 and reached 400,000 in 1999.

Thus, asylum has become one of the main methods of immigration into the EU. Many of the applications for asylum have been from people ostensibly fleeing from 'ethnic cleansing' in places such as Bosnia in the early 1990s and Kosovo in the late 1990s. Also many 'economic migrants' have been tempted to use the asylum process, seeing it as probably their best chance of success. United Nations data for 1999 show that, for all asylum cases judged that year, 9.2% were accepted in Germany, 9.8% in Italy, 15.6% in the Netherlands and 61.6% in Britain. In the EU as a whole 40% of all applications were rejected. The top six countries from which British asylum-seekers came in 1999 were China, Somalia, Sri Lanka, former Yugoslavia, Poland and Afghanistan. As yet there is no common EU policy on refugees although the 15 member nations have agreed to work towards one.

A recent European Commission publication (1998) suggests that refugees act like economic migrants in terms of destination within the EU. Most are attracted by an established community of their own nationality. However, other reasons that may be responsible for the choice of destination include the preferred routes of traffickers and the availability of direct flights.

Overall, refugees are not a heavy burden on taxpayers although this may not be how it seems in areas of high refugee density, such as the port of Dover. Here migrants share services such as schools, hospitals and housing with the poorest members of the established population. In such areas tensions can sometimes rise when a particularly large number of newcomers arrive. An interesting example is Ireland, whose experience of international migration has up to very recently been one of mass export. However, the strength of the 'celtic tiger' economy over the last decade has made Ireland an attractive destination, with asylum applications rising from 39 in 1992 to 4600 in 1998. Although the numbers appear relatively small to people in other countries, immigration has become a significant issue in Ireland.

Throughout the EU, individual governments have been trying to reduce the inflow of refugees while trying to distinguish genuine asylum seekers from purely 'economic migrants'. In 1993 Germany tightened its previously liberal asylum legislation, after accepting more than 60% of all those who applied for asylum in the EU in 1992. The new 'safe third country' rule means that if a person has passed through a country which Germany deems safe, he or she cannot apply for asylum in Germany. As Germany considers all neighbouring countries as safe, asylum seekers who do not arrive by air are likely to be rejected. The fall in the number of asylum applications in Germany prompted other nations to follow. For example, the Dutch government has recently devised a new Aliens Act, coming into effect in 2001. Applications will be processed much quicker and all asylum seekers who are eligible to stay will be given a more temporary status. Instead of giving full refugee status after the initial procedure each case will be reviewed after three years, and only then approved or rejected.

In Italy, the main concerns are what to do with the large number of illegal immigrants already in the country, and how to reduce the large scale trafficking of migrants, many brought in by speed-boat from Albania. Because many migrants use Italy only as a port of entry, the number of asylum applications is relatively small. This is also helped by the fact that:

1. Many refugees are given work permits on humanitarian grounds and thus do not need to apply for asylum.
2. Periodic amnesties for illegal immigrants means that they can regularise their situation rather than apply for refugee status.

France and Spain also receive relatively few asylum-seekers compared to the Netherlands, Britain and Germany.

It is likely that the migratory pressure on the EU will continue into the foreseeable future. The pressure will only abate in the long term if the EU, along with other MEDCs: provides more development aid, is more generous in terms of debt relief, acts to ensure that the terms of trade between MEDCs and LEDCs are fairer to the latter, and allocates more resources to preventing conflict in the world's trouble spots.

However, not all observers see immigration as a problem. There is a growing awareness among the general population that Europe's population is set to fall over the next 50 years. For example, it has been estimated that Italy's population, due to an extremely low birth rate, will drop by an alarming 28% by 2050. If Germany is to keep its working population stable between now and 2050, at current birth and death rates, it would need to import 487,000 migrants a year (United Nations Population Division). France would need 109,000 and the EU as a whole 1.6 million. If the objective is to keep the ratio of workers to pensioners steady, the inflow will need to be much higher. It is not just a matter of a falling working population, increasingly EU citizens do not want to undertake jobs which are heavy, dirty, dangerous and low paid. For example in February 2000 Spain's minister for employment stated 'We need people to do the jobs Spaniards no longer want to do'. If immigration is not to be the answer here, what are the alternatives? The main options appear to be to:

- encourage more women into the workplace
- improve training for the unemployed
- raise the retirement age or make it more profitable for retired people to work part-time
- reduce the school-leaving age for those taking up trade apprenticeships
- rely on technological advance to reduce the demand for labour in a significant number of occupations.

In 2003 five new countries will join the EU – the Czech Republic, Hungary, Estonia, Poland and Slovenia. There is particular concern in Germany and Austria that this will result in a high rate of immigration as the EU allows free movement within its borders. The Migration Research Unit at University College London estimates that the outflow from the five new members to the rest of the EU will be between 55,000 and 278,000 people each year. In order to stem the possibility of such a sudden large scale movement member countries have called for a transition period on labour migration from the five new members.

The International Centre for Migration Policy Development, based in Vienna, estimates that 400,000–500,000 illegal migrants enter the EU each year. If the true figure is indeed within this range it means that the scale of illegal immigration is higher than in the USA. However, it is acknowledged that a certain proportion of illegal immigration is accounted for by 'cross-border commuters' who shuttle back and forth between, for example, Germany and Poland. Seasonal migration into the EU is also important. For example in Britain 10,000 seasonal workers are recruited each year under an official scheme to import farm hands. This involves temporary migrants from countries such as Latvia, the Ukraine, Poland and the Czech Republic who are allowed to stay only between April and November. Although low in British terms, the wages on offer are so favourable compared to rates in their country of origin that there is no shortage of applicants. It is not just the wage rates that put off British workers but also the nature of the work which is increasingly viewed as 'undesirable'. Apart from the legal inflow of seasonal workers, illegal workers are also recruited by networks of traffickers.

c) Japan: A new attitude to immigration?

Compared with most other MEDCs Japan has a very small foreign population. In 1997 foreign labour accounted for only 0.2% of the work force compared with, for example 3.6% in Britain, 6.1% in France, and 9.1% in Germany. The reason is that Japan has kept an exceptionally tight rein on immigration. Only *nikkeijin*, or foreigners of Japanese descent may work in Japan as unskilled labourers while a raft of regulations restricts the inflow of skilled workers to a trickle. Illegal workers are pursued vigorously and deported. During the boom of the 1980s illegal immigrants were tolerated if they were prepared to do heavy, dirty and dangerous jobs. These immigrants helped to increase Japan's foreign-born population which has doubled in the past 20 years.

A growing number of decision makers in Japan want the current regulations to be eased. In key areas, particularly information technology Japan has a considerable shortage of skilled workers. It could compete with the USA and Europe to attract computer programmers from countries such as India and China, but most of these potential immigrants would not meet Japan's tough entry requirements which demand a university degree or ten years' relevant experience. At the other end of the scale, due to the relatively low wages on offer, Japan is short of low-skilled nursing assistants. This is another occupation where a higher rate of immigration could potentially solve the problem. As Japan's population rapidly ages the demand for labour will undoubtedly increase. According to a United Nations report published in 2000 Japan is ageing so quickly that it will need to import over 600,000 workers annually until 2050 to keep its working population stable. Attitudes in the country are such that there would be very little support for such a marked policy change.

d) The Philippines: The role of government in international labour migration

For a number of countries the export of 'surplus' labour is a key component of their overall economic development strategy. Nowhere is such a strategy more advanced and well organised than in the Philippines, the largest exporter of government-sponsored labour in the world. Within the Philippines, a programme of overseas employment as an economic development strategy has led to the growth of a complex agglomeration of government and private institutions that play a decisive role in the organisation and regulation of international labour migration.

In 1975 just over 36,000 workers were processed for overseas employment. Over the next two decades numbers increased sharply, reaching 500,000 in 1989 and 700,000 in 1994. In the latter year Filipino workers were employed in over 160 countries, with significant concentrations in the more industrialised countries of East Asia (i.e. Japan, Singapore, Taiwan) and in the oil-producing countries of the Middle East. The Philippines ranks first in the global provision of seafarers, providing approximately 16% of the world's total of 1.2 million. According to Tyner (2000) the production of formal contract labour migration in the Philippines consists of three levels of social organisation which link origins and destinations. These are:

• Contract procurement which involves negotiations between labour recruiters, foreign employers and government officials. It is at this level that labour-importing firms such as transnational corporations (TNCs) and hospitals state their labour requirements.
• Labour recruitment which consists of labour recruitment firms, government officials and worker applicants.
• Worker deployment whereby potential migrants, often as a result of a household decision, accept or reject an employment contract.

Under the 1974 Philippine Labour Code, all labour policies, including the export of labour, were to be realigned with overall economic growth and development goals. It was envisaged that the overseas employment programme would reduce domestic unemployment and underemployment, increase the skill level of migrant workers, and improve the balance of payments situation through remittances. Two agencies were created in 1974; the Overseas Employment Development Board (OEDB) and the National Seaman's Board (NSB), which would work with the already existing Bureau of Employment Services (BES). In 1982 these three organisations were combined to form the Philippines Overseas Employment Administration (POEA). The POEA was expected to improve the efficiency of the labour export programme and to increase the destination list and range of occupations of labour migrants. In order to achieve these goals it was recognised that the role of private recruitment agencies would become more and more important. Many recruitment agencies specialise in specific occupations such as nurses or construction workers.

The Philippines maintains a network of labour attachés in the principal labour-importing countries. The labour attachés and all other government officials working abroad are expected to be alert to any new labour market developments such as speculation about hotels or airports in the planning stages. All information is passed to the POEA. Over the years the POEA's marketing strategy has become increasing sophisticated, one of the reasons that 'Philippine workers' are generally perceived as a high quality product.

Within the Philippines the organisation of international migrant labour is almost entirely based in Manila, making the city a key location on the international labour circuit.

Case study: The USA – international migration

Immigration has had a phenomenal influence on the demographic history of the USA. Since 1820 almost 60 million people have entered the country (Figure 27). During this time both the rate of entry and the origin of immigrants have changed considerably. The highest recorded rate for any decade was 10.4 per thousand from 1901 to 1910, when 8.75 million newcomers arrived, although some decades in the nineteenth century were not far behind in proportional terms. The high rate of immigration continued until the outbreak of hostilities in Europe in 1914, whereupon it sharply abated from 12.3 per 1000 in 1914 to 3.2 per 1000 in 1915. It has rarely risen above the latter figure since, apart from a few exceptional years in the early 1920s and in recent years. The main reason for this is a growing concern among the American public about the numbers and origin of migrants.

In 1924 a system of 'national origins quotas' was introduced which operated with only slight modification until 1965. This legislation was designed to reduce migration significantly and, in

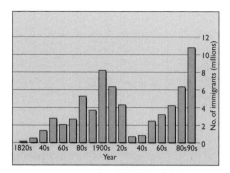

Figure 27 Legal immigrants in the USA
Source: The Economist: 11 March 2000

particular, to stem the influx of eastern and southern Europeans who entered the USA in extremely large numbers at the turn of the twentieth century. Anti-Chinese restrictions had already been in force for many years to fence off Chinese contract labourers. In fact Asian-Americans had to wait until the middle of the twentieth century before they were entitled to vote. The new system aimed to preserve the ethnic balance which existed in the country at the time of the 1920 Census, offered the largest quotas of entry permits to British, Irish and German immigrants (70% in total).

The racist overtones of this system, resulting in considerable internal and international opposition, led to its abolition in 1965. The 1965 Act, which became fully effective in July 1968, set an annual limit of 120,000 immigrants from the Western Hemisphere (the Americas) and 170,000 from the Eastern Hemisphere. People from every country within each hemisphere now had an equal chance of acceptance. However, immigration has exceeded this level considerably because relatives of US citizens are admitted without numerical limitation. The Immigration Act of 1990 raised immigration quotas by 40%.

As the intervening obstacles were lowered for potential migrants from a number of world regions, so the ethnic composition of new arrivals changed significantly. Europe, the previous major source region, has been overtaken since 1970 by the rest of the Americas and by Asia, a trend that is likely to continue in the future (Figure 28). The considerable increase in immigration in the 1990s, coinciding with a period of intense economic recession, reopened the immigration debate in the USA in a big way. By the late 1990s about one million immigrants were entering the USA each year. This comprised 730,000 legal immigrants, 200,000 illegal aliens, and 100,000 refugees. About 70% of legal immigrants are allowed in for the purposes of family reunifica-

Figure 28 San Francisco is home to a large Chinese community
centred around the Chinatown district

tion. Between 1990 and 2000, the number of foreign-born
American residents increased by 6 million to just over 25 million.
Half of the 50 million new inhabitants expected in America in
the next 25 years will be immigrants or the children of immigrants.

The inflow of migrants into the USA during the 1980s and
1990s has been termed 'the second great migration of the twentieth century'. One of its main consequences was the gradual
change in ethnic balance. According to the 1950 census America
was 89% white and 10% black with other races making a minor
contribution. In 1970 the main minority populations were blacks
(12%), Latinos (5%) and Asians (1%). Now Latinos account for

around 12% of the population, and if current trends continue, in 20 years' time they will dominate Texas and California. The most recent projection for 2050 is 26% Latino, 14% Black and 8% Asian.

Among other things, immigrants are helping to move the country's demographic centre of gravity south-westward as immigration into the USA is very spatially selective. In 1995, 55% of all immigration was to just four states – California, New York, Florida and Texas. There are three main reasons for this concentration. First, the location of existing immigrant communities which are well established in these states. Second, the availability of employment as these are the four most populous states in the country. Finally, the land border with Mexico for California and Texas and Florida's proximity to Caribbean countries. In 1997 over a quarter of Californians were born outside the USA. For Los Angeles the figure was almost 40%. This compares with 16% for New York, the next highest immigrant state, and 9.5 % for the USA as a whole.

a) Immigration categories

Most immigrants fall into the following categories:
- Family members account for two-thirds of immigrants.
- In theory 140,000 employment-related Green Cards (work permits) are available each year. However, in recent years this number has fallen due to a backlog in applications being processed by the Immigration and Naturalisation Service. There is pressure from industries such as information technology, where there is a considerable skills shortage, to increase the number of Green Cards issued. Congress increased the number of 'temporary' visas from 65,000 to 115,000 a year in 1998 in an effort to ease the skills shortages problem.
- America has a very good record for accepting refugees although there has been criticism that the rules do not always seem to be applied equally to different ethnic groups. All Cubans arriving in America are allowed to stay while, for example, Haitians are not. In 1999, only 38% of all those seeking asylum received it.
- An additional 50,000 Green Cards are allocated each year in a lottery for which about 7 million people apply. There is a limit to the number of applications from any particular country.
- There is a very high rate of illegal immigration into the USA. Because of its nature it is very difficult to assess the scale of illegal entry. The Immigration and Naturalisation Service put the figure in 1996 at 5 million. The largest number of illegal immigrants are from Mexico (2.7 million), followed by El Salvador (335,000), Guatemala (165,000), Canada (120,000), and Haiti (105,000).

b) The benefits and costs of immigration to the USA

The general attitude to immigration in the USA has always been much more positive than in Europe, although significant opposition does exist. There has also been a great deal of debate about the degree of economic advantage from immigration.

Various attempts have been made to quantify the economics of immigration of which the following are the most recent:

- A study carried out for Congress by the National Academy of Sciences (NAS) in 1997 concluded that immigration provided a net benefit to the American economy of around $10 billion a year in an economy worth $8 trillion. The NAS study calculated that competition from immigrants resulted in a 3% cut in wages of locals who had only a high-school certificate, with the worst-hit group usually being immigrants from the previous wave.
- An OECD survey published in 1997 concluded that immigration is financially beneficial to the American economy in the long term. Immigrants themselves take more out of the economy than they put in. For example, foreign born residents are 35% more likely to receive public assistance than native-born residents and the former, on average, pay 32% less in tax during their lifetimes than the latter. The payback comes with the children of immigrants who, on average, pay far more to the state in taxes than they take from it. However, it takes 40 years after an immigrant enters the country, the OECD calculates, before the financial gain to the state outweighs the cost. For the public purse, the most lucrative immigrant is a 21 year old with a higher-level education.
- Harvard economist George Borjas in his recent book Heaven's Door argues that the economic benefits brought by the latest 20-year wave of immigrants are less than for the immigration period 1950 to 1970 due to a fall off in levels of skill. He proposes that the USA should admit only 500,000 immigrants each year and select the most highly skilled. Borgas argues that rich Americans gain most from immigration. At home they gain from cheap nannies, cleaners and gardeners while if they own businesses, many benefit from relatively cheap immigrant labour. However, for the native-born poor the arrival of unskilled workers has made it harder to find jobs in an economy that demands even more education.
- The New Immigrant Survey Pilot published by the Rand Corporation in 1999 reached a different conclusion with regard to the skill level of immigrants. This study of legal immigrants only, found that the newcomers' median length of schooling was 13 years, one year more than for the native population, and that new immigrants were more highly educated than their predecessors.

However, it should be noted that the Borgas study included both legal and illegal immigrants.

The overall conclusion from the various recent studies is that in the long term the USA gains from immigration but that the immigrants gain even more.

Business in America generally favours immigration because:

- It has a general deflationary impact on wage rates by increasing the pool of labour particularly in the semi-skilled and unskilled areas.
- Without immigration some industries such as high technology would face severe skill shortages. One in four new businesses in Silicon Valley is started by someone of Indian or Chinese origin.
- Some industries, such as agriculture in California. rely on large scale employment of illegal immigrants.

As the number of immigrants has increased in recent years so has their political clout. Of the two main political parties the Republicans have wanted more control on immigration over the years but, as the number of immigrant voters has risen, the rhetoric has been toned down.

c) Still a melting pot?

The term 'melting pot' originated from a play of that name, written by Israel Zangwill, which opened in Washington in 1908; 'America is God's Crucible, the great Melting Pot where all the races of Europe are melting and reforming ... Germans and Frenchmen, Irishmen and Englishmen, Jews and Russians – into the Crucible with you all! God is making the American!' The analogy was that the USA would fuse together a diversity of cultures and create a typically American way of life.

Many observers are cynical about the validity of the melting pot theory of majority–minority relations. This has sometimes been expressed by the formula:

$$A + B + C = A$$

where A, B and C represent different ethnic groups and A is the dominant one. Over time the other groups gradually conform to the attitudes, values and lifestyle of the dominant group while A will change only marginally. In a major challenge to the melting pot theory Charles Truxillo, a professor of Chicano (Latino) studies at the University of New Mexico recently predicted that before the end of the twenty-first century California, southern Colorado, Texas, Arizona and New Mexico would separate from the USA to form a new sovereign Hispanic nation.

Assimilation into the host community is of major importance both to immigrants themselves and to native-born Americans. A 1999 study by the National Immigration Forum analysed four measures of assimilation – home ownership, citizenship, learning English and intermarriage – and concluded that recent immigrants are following much the same pattern as previous generations. As other studies have found, attitudes become more Americanised with each succeeding generation. A recent poll by the Washington Post of 2500 Latinos showed that nine out of ten recent arrivals think it is important to change to fit in but a similar proportion also think it is important to retain part of their culture. These attitudes are similar to previous ethnic groups who have entered the USA in large numbers.

Summary

- International migration is thought to be at its highest ever level.
- The attitudes to immigration, and the controls on it are subject to change over time.
- Large migrant communities are often established by one or a small number of initial migrants. Once a migrant culture is established in a donor community it tends to be self-perpetuating.
- The weight of evidence is that immigration is of economic benefit to receiving countries, at least in the long term.
- Immigration can have a substantial impact on the population structures of both receiving and donor countries.
- Social assimilation is a longer term process than economic assimilation. Political assimilation takes the longest of all.
- MEDCs often find it difficult to differentiate between economic migrants and refugees.
- Remittances can be so important to a donor country that some governments, such as in the Philippines, play a pivotal role in the process of emigration.
- There is considerable doubt about the economic benefits to home communities of return migrants.
- For many MEDCs immigration might be the only solution to working populations declining in number.
- In the USA the balance of evidence is that immigration has been of economic benefit to the country. However, the melting pot theory is being viewed with increasing cynicism.
- Immigration into the USA is very spatially selective.

Questions

1. Study Figure 26
   a Explain the difference between individual and social benefits from migration.
   b For emigrant countries, explain (i) social benefits 3 and 4 (ii) social costs 1 and 2.
   c For immigrant countries, explain (i) social benefit 2 (ii) individual cost 1 (iii) social cost 2.
   d With reference to examples, describe the impact of international migration on the population structures of donor and receiving countries.
2. Read the section on South Africa.
   a Why are there so many undocumented foreign migrants in South Africa?
   b Suggest why many South African companies are in favour of a high volume of migrant labour.
   c Why are many South African citizens against the entry of migrant workers from neighbouring countries?
   d What are the reasons for the high level of emigration from South Africa?
3. Read the section on the Philippines.
   a Why did the Philippines develop a programme of overseas employment?
   b What are the main destinations and occupations of Filipino migrant workers?
   c Describe the organisation of migrant labour in the Philippines.
   d Assess the individual costs and benefits of labour migration to Filipino workers who choose to seek employment abroad.
4. Read the case study on the USA.
   a Describe the changes in the volume of immigration into the USA since the 1820s.
   b To what extent have immigration restrictions changed over time?
   c Differentiate between the categories of immigrants in the USA.
   d What is the evidence that immigration is of economic benefit to the USA?
   e Discuss the concept of the 'melting pot'.

7 Refugees

KEY WORDS

Refugee: a person who has been forced to leave home and country because of 'a well-founded fear of persecution' on account of race, religion, social group or political opinion.

Internally displaced person: someone who has been forced to leave his/her home for reasons similar to a refugee but who remains in the same country.

UNHCR: the United Nations High Commissioner for Refugees.

1 The establishment of the UNHCR

Most religions encompass concepts such as sanctuary, refuge and asylum for people who are in distress. This is not surprising as there have been so many examples over time of people forced to flee their homes and seek refuge elsewhere. Modern European history documents the plight of the Hugenots, the Jews, the Czechs and Hungarians. But until the twentieth century no universal standards for the protection of such people existed. The issue of refugees was not regarded as an international problem until the League of Nations came into being after the First World War. The League appointed a number of High Commissioners and envoys to deal with specific refugee groups, but by 1950 the international community had still to establish a network of institutions, systems and laws to deal with the refugee problem in a global manner. On 14 December 1950, the United Nations General Assembly adopted the Statute of the United Nations High Commissioner for Refugees. The following year witnessed the adoption of the UN Convention Relating to the Status of Refugees. According to the Convention of 1951, refugees are people who have been forced to leave home and country because of 'a well-founded fear of persecution' on account of their race, religion, their social group or political opinions.

The United Nations High Commissioner for Refugees (UNHCR) is responsible for guaranteeing the security of refugees in the countries where they seek asylum and aiding the governments of these nations in this task. The UNHCR began as a small organisation with a three year mandate to help resettle European refugees who were still homeless after World War Two. Since then its role has widened significantly. From the 1960s to the late 1980s most of the UNHCR's work was in the LEDCs but in more recent years the collapse of the Soviet Union and the disintegration of Yugoslavia have drawn the

UNHCR back to Europe. In the 1900s UNHCR spent over $1 billion a year on its operations. However, the total expenditure on the refugee problem goes beyond this with the efforts of non-governmental organisations (NGOs) and the actions of individual countries.

The scale of the problem

Political upheaval and armed conflict, as well as natural disasters, have resulted in a huge number of people on the move over the last 20 years. In the twentieth century as a whole it is estimated that some 150 million people have been displaced.

During the last decade of the twentieth century governments, international organisations and the general public have been made much more aware of the plight of refugees and internally displaced persons through live television images from places such as Bosnia-Herzegovina, Chechnya, Iraq, Kosovo and Rwanda.

Originally the UNHCR commitments did not include the internally displaced. However, in 1999 it aided 4.1 million people in this situation (Figure 29). It is also concerned with supervising conditions for the return of refugees to their home countries. According to the UNHCR the total number of people dealt with by this body increased from 12 million in 1987 to 27.4 million in 1995, falling back to 22.3 million in 1999. In recent years the number of conventional refugees has actually fallen as the problem of external displacement has diminished in scale. However the problem of internal displacement has become worse.

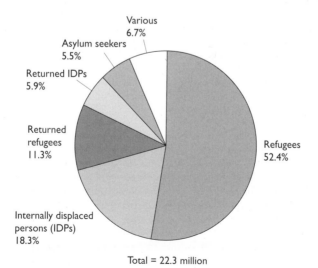

Total = 22.3 million

Figure 29 Total population of concern to UNHCR (1999)
Source: The State of the World's Refugees, UNHCR (2000)

Figure 30 Major refugee populations (1999)
Source: The State of the World's Refugees, UNHCR (2000)

Algeria

There are some 165,000 refugees from Western Sahara, according to estimates by the Algerian government, who are living in camps in the Tindouf region of southwestern Algeria.

Armenia and Azerbaijan

As a result of the conflict between Armenia and Azerbaijan in the early 1990s, there are nearly 300,000 Azerbaijani refugees in Armenia and nearly 190,000 Armenian refugees in Azerbaijan. Armenia hosts more refugees per capita than any other country in the world.

China

There are over 290,000 recognized refugees in China, virtually all of whom are from Viet Nam. Most are ethnic Chinese who have been in China since 1979.

Democratic Republic of the Congo

As well as generating over 250,000 refugees, the Democratic Republic of the Congo hosts some 285,000 refugees from neighbouring countries. These include, amongst others, some 150,000 Angolans, 68,000 Sudanese, 33,000 Rwandans, 19,000 Burundians and 12,000 from the Republic of the Congo.

Ethiopia

Ethiopia hosts nearly 260,000 refugees, including over 180,000 Somalis, some 70,000 Sudanese, and around 5,000 Kenyan refugees.

Federal Republic of Germany

The German government estimates that it hosts almost one million refugees – the largest number of refugees of any country in Western Europe. However, not all of these have been granted Convention refugee status. Most of those who have arrived over the past 10 years have come from the former Yugoslavia, Turkey, Iraq and Iran.

Guinea and Côte d'Ivoire

Despite being one of the poorest countries in Africa, Guinea continues to host some 370,000 refugees from Sierra Leone and some 130,000 from Liberia. Côte d'Ivoire hosts some 136,000 Liberian refugees.

India

India accommodates a large and varied refugee population including around 100,000 Tibetans, 66,000 Sri Lankans, 15,000 Bhutanese and 14,000 Afghans. Like other countries in the region, India is not party to the 1951 UN Refugee Convention or the 1967 Protocol and does not give UNHCR access to all the refugees on its territory.

Indonesia

As a result of the violence which erupted at the time of the vote for independence in East Timor in 1999, some 280,000 people fled from East Timor to West Timor, in Indonesia. Although many subsequently returned, some 163,000 refugees remained in Indonesia in December 1999.

Thailand

Thailand hosts nearly 100,000 refugees from Myanmar. Although Thailand does not regard these people officially as refugees, it does permit UNHCR and other humanitarian organizations to assist them.

Federal Republic of Yugoslavia

The Federal Republic of Yugoslavia hosts some 500,000 refugees, the largest refugee population in the region. The refugee population includes around 300,000 Croatian refugees and some 200,000 refugees from Bosnia and Herzegovina.

Zambia

Zambia hosts over 160,000 Angolan refugees. It also hosts some 36,000 refugees from the Democratic Republic of the Congo.

Nepal

There are over 100,000 Bhutanese refugees in Nepal. Many have been there for more than a decade. Nepal is also host to some 20,000 Tibetans.

Iran and Pakistan

Iran and Pakistan continue to host the largest refugee population for which UNHCR has responsibility – the Afghans. From a peak of 6.2 million in 1990, there are now over 2.5 million Afghan refugees. This includes 1.3 million in Iran and 1.2 million in Pakistan. There are also over 500,000 Iraqi refugees in Iran which, with a total of over 1.8 million refugees, hosts the largest number of refugees in the world.

The Palestinians

The Palestinians are the world's largest refugee population and over the past 50 years have spread all over the world. Some 3.6 million remain concentrated in Jordan, Syria, Lebanon, Gaza and the West Bank. The UN Relief and Works Agency (UNRWA) has responsibility for providing assistance to these refugees.

Kenya and Uganda

Kenya hosts some 224,000 refugees. The largest groups are Somalis (some 140,000) and Sudanese (some 64,000). Uganda hosts nearly 220,000 refugees, including some 200,000 Sudanese.

Sudan

Sudan hosts over 390,000 refugees, including over 340,000 Eritreans and some 35,000 Ethiopians. Most of the Eritrean refugees have been in Sudan since before Eritrea gained independence in 1993. Sudan has also produced some 475,000 refugees as a result of its long-running civil war, most of whom are in Uganda, Ethiopia, the Democratic Republic of the Congo and Kenya.

United Republic of Tanzania

With a total of over 620,000 refugees, Tanzania hosts the largest refugee population in Africa. This refugee population comprises some 500,000 Burundians, nearly 100,000 from the Democratic Republic of Congo and some 20,000 Rwandans.

Figure 30 shows the major refugee populations worldwide in 1999 according to the UNHCR. 2.5 million Afghans, almost equally split between Iran and Pakistan, make up the largest refugee group in the world for which the UNHCR has responsibility. However 3.6 million Palestinians form an even larger group whose welfare is the remit of the UN Relief and Works Agency (UNRWA). Over 80% of refugees are in LEDCs. More than half are children and most of the adults are women. Adult males tend to be under-represented in refugee populations, often because they are engaged in other activities, whether farming, working in another location, fighting in an army or rebel group, or visiting their country of origin to prepare for the repatriation of their family.

2 The complexity of forced displacement

Forced displacement is a complex phenomenon which assumes many different forms. A 1996 conference addressing migration and displacement in the former Soviet Union drew international attention to no fewer than nine categories of uprooted people in the former Soviet Union. The conference identified refugees, people in refugee-like situations, internally displaced people, repatriants, formerly deported peoples, transit migrants, illegal migrants, ecological migrants and involuntarily relocating persons. In recent years forced population displacements have been perceived as an increasingly important element of national and regional security. Large scale displacements of people has prompted other states and regional organisations to deploy their armed forces as witnessed in countries such as Albania, Iraq, Liberia, Somalia and the former Yugoslavia. Forcibly displaced people are faced with mounting rejection when they attempt to seek safety elsewhere. A number of trends appear to have contributed to the growing scale and speed of forced displacement:

- The emergence of new forms of warfare involving the destruction of whole social, economic and political systems.
- The spread of light weapons and land mines, available at prices which enable whole populations to be armed.
- The use of mass evictions and expulsions as a weapon of war and as a means of establishing culturally and ethnically homogeneous societies.

In a number of locations around the world, whole regions have become affected by interlocking and mutually reinforcing patterns of armed conflict and forced displacement, for example in the Caucasus and central Africa. The UNHCR has noted a growing number of situations in which people are repeatedly uprooted, expelled or relocated within and across state borders, forcing them to live a desperately insecure and nomadic existence. The UNHCR has observed that 'the forced displacement of minorities, including depopulation and repopulation tactics in support of territorial claims and self-determination, has become an abominable characteristic of the contemporary world.'

The main reasons for the new refugee crisis stem from the closing of frontiers, and the aims of some nations to expel certain sectors of the population. Even though 10 million people have returned to their homes since 1990, the number of displaced persons who remain trapped in war zones is growing. However, there are some positive trends. Since the beginning of the 1990s, many longstanding conflicts have come to an end or have significantly reduced in intensity, allowing millions of refugees and internally displaced people to return home.

There have been increasing examples of safety during asylum being threatened. This has occurred through armed attacks on refugee camps, the forced recruitment of young men into military forces, sexual violence inflicted upon displaced women and girls and displaced people being forced back to their country of origin, often to conditions that are far from safe.

a) Environmental catastrophe and human displacement

Ecological and environmental change are a common cause of human displacement. A number of examples can be found in the former Soviet states of central Asia. Much of central Asia is affected by problems such as soil degradation and desertification, a situation created by decades of agricultural exploitation, industrial pollution and overgrazing. The worst situation is in and around the Aral Sea, a large lake located between Kazakstan and Uzbekistan. In a large scale effort to increase cotton production in the region, most of the river water flowing into the Aral Sea was siphoned off for irrigation. Since 1960 the surface area of the sea has been reduced by half. Dust from the dried-up bed of the sea, containing significant amounts of agricultural and industrial chemicals, is carried long distances by the wind adding further to the pollution, salinization and desertification of the land. Agricultural production has fallen sharply and food has increased in price; the fishing industry has been almost totally destroyed and local people are plagued by significant health problems. It has been estimated that more than 100,000 people have left the Aral Sea area since 1992 because of these problems.

Semipalatinsk in Kazakstan, where almost 500 nuclear bombs were exploded between 1949 and 1989, 150 of them above ground, is another environmental disaster zone. 160,000 people decided to leave this area due to concerns about the consequences of nuclear radiation. Around half of these people moved to other parts of Kazakstan with the remainder going to a number of other former Soviet states.

Refugees can have a considerable impact on the environment. They often concentrate in marginal and vulnerable environments where the potential for environmental degradation is high. Apart from immediate problems concerning sanitation and the disposal of waste, long term environmental damage may result from deforestation associated with the need for firewood and building materials. Increased pressure on the land can result in further soil degradation.

b) Mass desperation

In addition to situations where virtually no choice exists but to move some authors attribute large scale population displacements, for example Albanians fleeing to Italy, to a form of mass desperation provoked by very rapid processes of social, economic and political change. Never before have people living in difficult conditions been more aware of the higher quality of life elsewhere. The process of economic polarisation which has seen the gap between rich and poor nations widen considerably, has an obvious relevance to migratory movements of a more voluntary nature. Some people, who see no chance of satisfying their aspirations in their own country and are unable to enter a higher income country by regular and legal means may be tempted to seek admission by submitting a claim for refugee status. MEDCs are finding it more and more difficult to distinguish between economic migrants and genuine refugees.

A recent UNHCR publication listed some of the difficulties and dilemmas which it and other humanitarian organisations have faced in recent years:

- To what extent have the world's most powerful states used humanitarian action as a substitute for the decisive political and military action that is sometimes required to bring armed conflicts to an end?
- How can the integrity and impartiality of humanitarian action be preserved in the increasingly political context in which it is undertaken?
- What action can be taken to protect and assist displaced and other war-affected populations, and what role can multinational military forces play in this task?
- Why are many traditionally generous asylum countries now closing their borders to displaced populations, and how can they be encouraged and assisted to provide refugees with a satisfactory degree of security?
- How can the civilian character of refugee camps be maintained, and what can be done to demilitarise those which have come under the control of armed groups?
- Under what conditions is it legitimate for humanitarian organisations to encourage or even insist upon the repatriation of refugee populations to their country of origin?
- How does the return and reintegration of displaced populations affect the broader process of peace building in countries which have experienced civil wars and communal conflicts?
- To what extent can refugees be distinguished from other migrants, and what kind of procedures can states establish to assess large numbers of

individual asylum applications in a fair, thorough and sufficiently speedy manner?

- How is the question of citizenship related to the problem of forced displacement, and how can governments be encouraged to refrain from actions which leave large numbers of people stateless and vulnerable to expulsion?

Summary

- The UNHCR, established in 1950, is responsible for guaranteeing the security of refugees.
- In 1997 the UNHCR took on a commitment to internally displaced people as well as refugees.
- Forced displacement is a complex phenomenon which assumes many different forms.
- The countries most affected by the refugee problem are the poorest in the world.
- Refugee populations are dominated by women and children. Adult males tend to be heavily under-represented because they are engaged in other activities.
- There have been increasing examples of safety during asylum being threatened.
- Ecological and environmental change are a common cause of human displacement.
- Refugees can have a considerable impact on the environment.

Questions

1.

   a Describe the composition of the total population of concern to UNHCR in 1999.

   b What is meant by the terms (i) refugee (ii) internally displaced person?

   c Suggest why the number of refugees was considerably higher in the 1990s than in the preceding decades.

   d Discuss the problems faced by refugees and internally displaced people.

   e Why do only a small number of asylum seekers gain entry to the country of their application?

References

J. Agesa and R. Agesa (1999) Gender differences in the Incidence of Rural to Urban Migration. Evidence from Kenya, *Journal of Development Studies*, Vol 35, number 6.

D.A. Ahlbury and R.P. Brown (1998) Migrants Intentions to Return Home and Capital Transfers: A Study of Tongans and Samoans in Australia, *Journal of Development Studies*, Vol 35, number 2.

T. Champion et al. (1996) *The Population of Britain in the 1990s: A Social and Economic Atlas*, Clarendon Press, Oxford.

A. de Haan (1999) Livelihoods and Poverty: The Role of Migration – A Critical Review of the Migration Literature, *The Journal of Development Studies*, 36, 1–47.

(2000) The United States: Immigration Survey', *The Economist*, 11.3.00.

(2000) Survey: China, *The Economist*, 8.4.00.

(2000) Europe's Immigrants: A Continent on the Move, *The Economist*, 6.5.00.

(2000) South Africa's Migrant Workers, *The Economist*, 2.9.00.

W.H. Frey and K.L. Liaw (1998) Immigrant Concentration and Domestic Migrant Dispersal: Its Movement to Nonmetropolitan Areas 'White Flight'?, *Professional Geographer*, 50, 215–232.

Focus on London 99 (1999), *The Stationery Office*.

P. Gober (2000) Immigration and North American Cities, *Urban Geography*, 21, 83–90.

B. Hall (2000) Immigration in the European Union: Problem or Solution, *OECD Observer*, No.221/222.

R. Hall (1989) *World Population Trends*, CUP.

R. Hall and P. White (1995) *Europe's Population; Towards the Next Century*, UCL Press.

D. Hare (1999) Push versus Pull Factors in Migration Outflows and Returns: Determinants of Migration Status and Spell Duration Among China's Rural Population, *The Journal of Development Studies*, 35, 45–72.

W. Hornby and M. Jones (1993) *Population Geography*, CUP.

J.A. Jackson (ed) (1969) *Migration*, CUP.

S. Jackson (1998) *Britain's Population: demographic issues in contemporary society*, Routledge.

V.A. Lawson (1988) Hierarchical Households and Gender Migration in Latin America: Feminist Extensions to Migration Research, *Progress in Human Geography*, 22, 39–53.

G.J. Lewis (2000) Changing Places in a Rural World: The Population Turnaround in Perspective, *Geography*, 85, 157–165.

T. Lynn Smith (1960) *Fundamentals of Population Study*, Philadelphia: Lippincott.

A.K. Matogunje (1970) Systems Approach to a Theory of Rural–Urban Migration, *Geographical Analysis*, 2.

G.A. Manson and R.E. Groop (2000) US Intercounty Migration in the 1990s: People and Income Move Down the Urban Hierarchy, *Professional Geographer*, 52.

K.E. McHugh (2000) Inside, Outside, Upside down, Backward, Forward, Round and Round: A Case for Ethnographic Studies in Migration, *Progress in Human Geography*, 24, 71–89.

P. Ogden (1990) *Migration and Geographical Change*, CUP.

M. Parnwell (1993) *Population Movements and the Third World*, Routledge, London.

B. Price and P. Guinness (1997) *North America: An Advanced Geography*, Hodder & Stoughton.

J. Shen (1996) Internal Migration and Regional Population Dynamics in China, *Progress in Planning, 45*.

J. Shen (1998) China's Future Population and Development Challenges, *The Geographical Journal, 164*, 32–40.

M.P. Todaro (1971) Income Expectations, Rural–Urban Migration and Employment in Africa, *International Labour Review 104*, 387–413.

J. Torpey (2000) *The Invention of the Passport*, CUP.

J.A. Tyner (2000) Global Cities and Circuits of Global Labour: The Case of Manila, Philippines, *Professional Geographer, 52*, 61–74.

United Nations High Commissioner for Refugees, *The State of the World's Refugees*, OUP. (2000).

P. White and R. Woods (eds) (1980) T*he Geographical Impact of Migration*, Longman, London.

W. Zelinski (1971) The hypothesis of the mobility transition, *Geographical Review 61*, 219–49.

G. K Zipf (1949) *Human Behaviour and the Principle of Least Effort*, Addison-Wesley, Reading, Massachusetts, USA.

Index

Afghanistan 36–7, 109
Africa 8, 17, 25, 27, 30, 34–5, 38, 45, 52, 54
Afro-Caribbean 2
Agesa, J. 51
agrarian reform 60–1
Ahlbury, D. 91
Algeria 87
Amazon 33, 42–3
Americas 2, 27–28, 30–3
approaches
 accommodative 58–9
 manipulative 59–60
 negative 56–8
 preventive 60–1
Arctic Circle 25
Asia 25, 27
Asian 2, 16, 45
assimilation 14–15, 17–18, 86
asylum seekers 37, 86, 93–6
Australia 2, 16, 17, 27, 33, 35–36, 38, 72–3

Bangladesh 45
black Americans 32
Brazil 15, 16, 31–3, 47, 59, 60, 71
Britain 2, 4, 11, 15, 38, 72–74, 84, 93–4
Brown, R. 91

Canada 16, 17, 28, 72–3
capitalism 45–6
Caribbean 31
census 22, 78
Chernobyl 8
China 3, 15, 17, 50, 55, 57, 61–7, 86
circulatory movements 4, 10
colonisation 25
counterurbanisation 2, 11, 39, 69, 72–4
Crete 30

De Hann, A. 1, 21, 51

demographic transition 10
destination 5
development 54–6
distance continuum 41–42
Dutch 34–5

Egypt 15, 16
emigration 1, 6
England 10, 22, 70
Ethiopia 45
ethnography 52, 86
Europe 10, 11, 25–28, 34–37, 93–96
evacuees 7

fertility 1
First World War 36
France 2, 16, 70
French 31

gender 21, 51–2
Germany 2, 16, 33, 38, 70, 72, 87, 93–5
Ghana 87
Giddens, A. 21
gravity model 12–13
Greece 30, 35
Greenland 28
green revolution 55
guestworkers 37, 87

Hagerstrand, T. 7
hominid 25
Homo sapiens 25

Ice Age 25, 27
immigration 1, 6, 33–6, 86–105
India 8, 36, 49, 50, 52, 55
Indians [American] 31
industrialisation 46, 69–70, 76–7
internally displaced people 6, 45, 106–12
Inuit 28
inverse distance law 12
Ireland 16, 72–3, 89

Italy 2, 33, 35, 94–95
Ivory Coast 87

Japan 22, 38, 70, 72, 96–7

Kenya 51

Lee, E. 13–17, 46
Lewis, G. 72–4
life cycle 5, 14, 17
London 70, 73, 83–4, 89

Mabogunje, A. 8, 17–19
macro-level 41, 45–6
Malaysia 59
Marxist theory 21
McHugh, K. 52
meso-level 41, 45–6
Mexico 15, 60, 90–1
micro-level 41, 49–50
Middle East 26, 28, 87
migrant culture 86, 90–2
migration
    chain 5, 49
    conservative 8
    counterstream 16
    data 22–3
    efficiency 4–5, 16
    forced 8, 30–1, 44
    free 8, 44
    gross 4, 6
    impelled 8
    in-migration 4, 6
    innovating 8
    internal 2–3, 4, 41–85
    international 2–4, 74–5,
        85–105
    mass 8, 10
    net 4, 6
    out 4, 6
    primitive 8
    rate 5
    relay 5
    rural–urban 7–10, 17, 19,
        38–9, 47–67
    step 5
    stream 5, 16, 41–2

theories 10–21
typologies 4, 7–10
urban–rural 7–8
volume 15–16

Minoan civilisation 30
mobility 4, 9–11
mortality 1, 28
Mountz, A. 90–91

natural disasters 8, 45
Neolithic revolution 28
New Guinea 27
New Towns 3, 77–80
Newton, I. 13
New Zealand 2, 27, 35, 72
Nigeria 87
North America 11, 37

Oceania 27–8, 35–36
OECD 88
origin 5

Pakistan 8, 59
Parnwell, M. 41–2, 44, 47, 53, 57
Peru 48–9, 51–2, 59
Petersen, W. 7–8, 44
Philippines 97–98
policies 56–67
population equation 1
population registers 22–3
population turnover 4
Portuguese 30–2
pull factors 5, 17
push factors 5, 17

Ravenstein, E. 11–12, 22
refugees 2, 6, 8, 106–112
remittances 21, 41, 53–5, 90–2
resettlement 7
reurbanisation 69
Romans 30
rural depopulation 2, 69, 71–2
Russia 33–4
Rwanda 38

Samoan islands 27, 91

Scandinavia 22, 27, 33
Second World War 36
service decline 2
Siberia 27, 33–4
Singh, A. 52
Smith, A. 11
Smith, L. 7
social surveys 22–3
South Africa 34–5, 59, 87, 92–3
South America 28, 33, 51–2
South Korea 60
Soviet Union 3, 37–8, 109–10
Spanish 30–1
Sri Lanka 60
Stark, H. 20–1
Stouffer, S. 13
structuralist theory 21
structuration theory 21
systems approach 17–19

Thailand 48, 59

Todaro, M. 19–20, 48–9, 51
Tonga 27, 91
Torpey, J. 87
Tokyo 71

UN 56
UNHCR 6, 36, 106–12
UNRWA 109
USA 2, 4, 15–16 , 28, 31–3, 70, 72–5, 86, 90–1, 98–106

Venezuela 59

Wright, R. 90–1

Yugoslavia 37–8, 109

Zelinski, W. 9–11
Zipf, G. 12